Mountain Biking on the
South Downs

About the Author

Peter Edwards grew up in Sussex and nurtured a love of walking and mountain biking amid the 'blunt, bow-headed, whale-backed' hills of the South Downs. He has undertaken numerous walking and cycling expeditions in Europe and beyond and is particularly drawn to wild and remote landscapes. *Mountain Biking on the South Downs* is his second Cicerone guide. Peter also writes about his walking and cycling trips on his blog site www.writesofway.com.

Other Cicerone guides by the author

Mountain Biking in Central and Southern Scotland
Mountain Biking on the North Downs
The Hebrides
Walking on Jura, Islay and Colonsay
Walking on Rum and the Small Isles

Mountain Biking on the
South Downs

by Peter Edwards

© Peter Edwards 2011
First edition 2011
ISBN: 978 1 85284 645 9
Reprinted 2014 (with updates),
2018 (with updates)

Published by Cicerone
Juniper House, Murley Moss
Oxenholme Road, Kendal
Cumbria LA9 7RL
www.cicerone.co.uk

Printed in China
on behalf of Latitude Press Ltd.
A catalogue record for this book is
available from the British Library.

All photographs are by the author
except those on pages 1, 27, 43,
100, 184, 192, 210, 220 and 221
(Andy Dodd); pages 2 and 22 (James
Stevenson) and pages 193, 196, 213
and 216 (Craig Shuttleworth).

Ordnance Survey® This product includes
mapping data
licensed from Ordnance Survey® with
the permission of the Controller of Her
Majesty's Stationery Office. © Crown
copyright 2014. All rights reserved.
Licence number PU100012932.

DEDICATION

For Andy Dodd – his energy and
enthusiasm know no bounds!

Front cover: Climbing Barnsfarm Hill
(Routes 14 and 16)
Title page: Climbing Windover Hill
(SDW, Day 3)
Back cover: On Balmer Huff (Route 20)

ACKNOWLEDGEMENTS

Thanks are due to Andy and Jen Dodd
for accompanying me on many of this
guidebook's 'research' rides. Thanks to
Sarah Blann, Finlay and Brodie McBride,
Bill Parslow and Janice Britz for putting
me up. Thanks to Andy Rayment, cycle
mechanic and osteopath, for fixing
my broken bikes and my broken body
and also for coining the term 'jungle-
biking'. Thanks to Craig Shuttlewood,
Nick Miles, James Stevenson and Pat
Doe for modelling and pictures. Special
thanks to the lovely Fiona Rintoul
for supporting and encouraging me
through the writing of this guidebook.

UPDATES TO THIS GUIDE

While every effort is made by our authors
to ensure the accuracy of guidebooks
as they go to print, changes can occur
during the lifetime of an edition. Any
updates that we know of for this guide
will be on the Cicerone website (www.
cicerone.co.uk/645/updates), so please
check before planning your trip. We
also advise that you check information
about such things as transport,
accommodation and shops locally. Even
rights of way can be altered over time.
We are always grateful for information
about any discrepancies between a
guidebook and the facts on the ground,
sent by email to updates@cicerone.
co.uk or by post to Cicerone, Juniper
House, Murley Moss, Oxenholme Road,
Kendal, LA9 7RL.

Register your book: To sign up to
receive free updates, special offers and
GPX files where available, register your
book at www.cicerone.co.uk.

Contents

INTRODUCTION   13

THE SOUTH DOWNS WAY NATIONAL TRAIL   27

ROUTES AROUND WINCHESTER   61

Routes around Arundel and Worthing   121

Routes around Brighton and Lewes   159

Routes around Eastbourne   203

Appendices   231

Emergencies

Always carry a charged mobile phone with you so that emergency services can be alerted in case of serious injury.

If you do need to report such an injury, first make a note of all relevant details including location (giving the grid reference if possible), the nature of the injury and your mobile phone number. Then call 999 and ask for both Police and Ambulance.

Be ready to give the location and nature of the incident and the numbers of any phones carried by the party. Do not change your position until you are contacted by the emergency services.

There are accident and emergency departments at Winchester, Chichester, Worthing, Brighton and Eastbourne. For more information on emergencies and mountain biking safely see the Safety section in the introduction.

Symbols used on OS maps

 main route/stage number

 start point/finish point

 start/finish point

→ direction of main route

 variant route/stage number

 alternative start point/finish point

 alternative start/finish point

 alternative start/finish stage

→ direction of variant/alternative route

 pub, café, water source

For full OS symbols key see OS maps.

Difficulty grades

■ medium

▲ hard

◆ very hard

Profile symbols

⇌ train station

🅿 car park

✕ path crossing/
junction

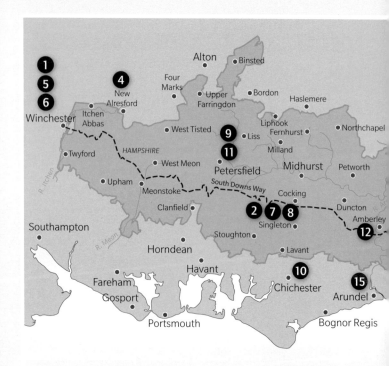

KEY

SOUTH DOWNS WAY NATIONAL TRAIL

Route 1 ▲ The South Downs Way Day 1
Winchester to Cocking

Route 2 ▲ The South Downs Way Day 2
Cocking to Ditchling Beacon

Route 3 ▲ The South Downs Way Day 3
Ditchling Beacon to Eastbourne

〰〰〰 South Downs Way
National Trail

ROUTES AROUND WINCHESTER

Route 4 ■ New Alresford – Warnford Circuit
Route 5 ▲ Winchester – Gander Down Circuit
Route 6 ▲ Winchester to Petersfield
♦ (return variants)

ROUTES AROUND
CHICHESTER AND PETERSFIELD

Route 7 ▲ Westdean Woods and Cocking Down
Route 8 ▲ Heyshott Down and Charlton Forest
Route 9 ▲ Petersfield – Beacon Hill Circuit
Route 10 ▲ Chichester – Charlton Forest Circuit
Route 11 ♦ Petersfield – Singleton Forest Circuit

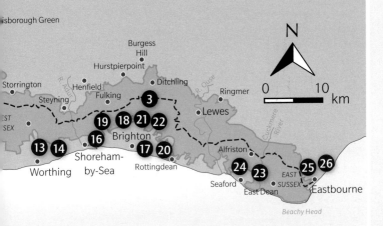

ROUTES AROUND ARUNDEL AND WORTHING

Route 12 ■ Amberley and Houghton Forest
Route 13 ■ Worthing – Chanctonbury Ring Circuit
Route 14 ▲ Worthing – Springhead Hill Circuit
Route 15 ◆ Arundel – Graffham Down Circuit (and Amberley alternative)
Route 16 ◆ Lancing – Amberley Mount Circuit

ROUTES AROUND BRIGHTON AND LEWES

Route 17 ■ Castle Hill Circuit
Route 18 ▲ Brighton – Lewes Circuit
Route 19 ▲ Brighton – Truleigh Hill Circuit
Route 20 ▲ Devil's Dyke – Blackcap Circuit
Route 21 ▲ Brighton to Eastbourne
Route 22 ◆ Brighton – Ouse Valley Circuit

ROUTES AROUND EASTBOURNE

Route 23 ■ Friston Forest Circuit
Route 24 ■ Seaford – Firle Beacon Circuit
Route 25 ▲ Eastbourne – Cuckmere Valley Circuit
Route 26 ◆ Eastbourne – Firle Beacon Circuit

No.	Route Title	Grade	% Off Road	Start
1	South Downs Way: Day one – Winchester to Cocking	▲	70%	Winchester train station SU 478 300
2	South Downs Way: Day two – Cocking to Ditchling Beacon	▲	95%	Cocking Hilltop car park SU 875 167
3	South Downs Way: Day three – Ditchling Beacon to Eastbourne	▲	85%	Ditchling Beacon car park TQ 333 130
4	New Alresford – Warnford Circuit	■	65%	Watercress Line scenic railway car park, New Alresford SU 589 325
5	Winchester – Gander Down Circuit	▲	65%	Winchester train station SU 478 300
6	Winchester to Petersfield (and return variants)	▲ (◆)	65%	Winchester train station SU 478 300
7	Westdean Woods and Cocking Down	▲	85%	Cocking Hilltop car park SU 875 167
8	Heyshott Down and Charlton Forest	▲	90%	Cocking Hilltop car park SU 875 167
9	Petersfield – Beacon Hill Circuit	▲	55%	Petersfield train station SU 744 236
10	Chichester – Charlton Forest Circuit	▲	95%	Chichester train station SU 858 044
11	Petersfield – Singleton Forest Circuit	◆	60%	Petersfield train station SU 744 236 or Harting Downs car park SU 791 180
12	Amberley and Houghton Forest	■	85%	Amberley train station TQ 026 118
13	Worthing – Chanctonbury Ring Circuit	■	80%	Worthing train station TQ 146 034
14	Worthing – Springhead Hill Circuit	▲	75%	Worthing train station TQ 146 034
15	Arundel – Graffham Down Circuit (and Amberley alternative)	◆	90%	Arundel train station TQ 024 064 or Amberley train station TQ 026 118
16	Lancing – Amberley Mount Circuit	◆	90%	Shoreham-by-Sea train station TQ 146 034 or Lancing Ring Nature Reserve TQ 183 063
17	Castle Hill Circuit	■	95%	Car park on B2123 Falmer Road TQ 356 063 or Brighton train station TQ 310 049
18	Brighton – Lewes Circuit	▲	90%	Stanmer Park TQ 343 087
19	Brighton – Truleigh Hill Circuit	▲	80%	Junction by the A27 TQ 303 096 or Brighton train station TQ 310 049
20	Devil's Dyke – Blackcap Circuit	▲	65%	Brighton train station TQ 310 049
21	Brighton to Eastbourne	▲	85%	Stanmer Park TQ 343 087
22	Brighton – Ouse Valley Circuit	◆	85%	Stanmer Park TQ 343 087
23	Friston Forest Circuit	■	65%	Seaford train station TV 482 992 or Exceat car park TV 518 996
24	Seaford – Firle Beacon Circuit	■	75%	Seaford train station TV 482 992
25	Eastbourne – Cuckmere Valley Circuit	▲	80%	Eastbourne train station TV 610 991
26	Eastbourne – Firle Beacon Circuit	◆	85%	Eastbourne train station TV 610 991 or Warren Hill TV 588 979

Finish	Distance	Ascent	Time	Page No
Cocking Hilltop car park SU 875 167	56.5km (35 miles)	1295m (4250ft)	4hrs 30mins–5hrs 30mins	29
Ditchling Beacon car park TQ 333 130	55.5km (34½ miles)	1395m (4580ft)	4hrs 30mins–5hrs 30mins	41
Eastbourne train station TV 609 991	46.5km (29 miles)	1020m (3345ft)	3hrs 30mins–4hrs 30 mins	53
Watercress Line scenic railway car park, New Alresford SU 589 325	29km (18 miles)	450m (1475ft)	2hrs–2hrs 30 mins	63
Winchester train station SU 478 300	30.5km (19 miles)	505m (1660ft)	2hrs 30mins–3hrs	69
Petersfield train station SU 743 235	52km (32½ miles); variants differ	890m (2930ft); variants differ	4–4hrs 30 mins; variants differ	75
Cocking Hilltop car park SU 875 167	21.5km (13½ miles) or 26.5km (16½ miles) with variant	515m (1690ft); 610m (2005ft) with variant	2–2hrs 30mins (add 30mins with variant)	89
Cocking Hilltop car park SU 875 167	18km (11 miles)	555m (1815ft)	2hrs–2hrs 30mins	95
Petersfield train station SU 744 236	38.5km (24 miles)	895m (2940m)	3hrs–4hrs	99
Chichester train station SU 858 044	42km (26 miles)	800m (2625ft)	3hrs–4hrs	107
Petersfield train station SU 744 236 or Harting Downs car park SU 791 180	54.5km (34 miles)	1310m (4290ft)	4–5hrs	113
Amberley train station TQ 026 118	15km (9½ miles)	380m (1255ft)	1hr–1hr 30mins	123
Worthing train station TQ 146 034	25km (15½ miles)	545m (1790ft)	2hrs–2hrs 30mins	127
Worthing train station TQ 146 034	41km (25½ miles)	810m (2555ft)	3hrs–3hrs 30mins	133
Arundel train station TQ 024 064 or Amberley train station TQ 026 118	47.5km (29½ miles); alternative: 36km (22½ miles)	1125m (3685ft); alternative: 940m (3090ft)	4hrs–5hrs	141
Shoreham-by-Sea train station TQ 146 034 or Lancing Ring Nature Reserve TQ 183 063	50.5km (31½ miles)	1090m (3580ft)	4hrs–5hrs	151
Car park on B2123 Falmer Road TQ 356 063 or Brighton train station TQ 310 049	16.5km (10 miles)	400m (1310ft)	1hr 30mins	161
Stanmer Park TQ 343 087	29.5km (18½ miles)	640m (2105ft)	2hrs 30mins–3hrs	167
Brighton Palace Pier TQ 313 039	29.5km (18½ miles)	520m (1715ft)	3hrs–3hrs 30mins	173
Brighton train station TQ 310 049	44km (27½ miles)	990m (3240ft)	3hrs 30mins–4hrs	181
Eastbourne train station TV 610 99	42.5km (26½ miles)	985m (3235ft)	3hrs 30mins–4hrs	189
Stanmer Park TQ 343 087	43km (27 miles)	990m (3240ft)	3hrs–4hrs	197
Seaford train station TV 482 992 or Exceat car park TV 518 996	22km (13¾ miles); 14.5km (9 miles) if starting at Exceat	510m (1675ft)	2hrs; 1hr 30mins if starting at Exceat	205
Seaford train station TV 482 992	28.5km (17¾ miles)	520m (1700ft)	2hrs–2hrs 30mins	211
Eastbourne train station TV 610 991	34km (21 miles)	815m (2675ft)	2hrs–3hrs	217
Eastbourne train station TV 610 991 or Warren Hill TV 588 979	46km (28½ miles)	1195m (3920ft)	3hrs 30mins–4hrs	223

Climbing chalk bridleway at Lullington Heath (Route 26)

Introduction

The South Downs are a mountain biker's paradise. Some of the finest off-road routes to be found anywhere are available in abundance amid the green, rolling chalk hills that comprise some of the UK's most subtly beautiful countryside. The Downs are criss-crossed by thousands of kilometres of well-maintained rights of way, including an estimated 1,473km (915 miles) of byways and bridleways open to mountain bikers. This vast network of trails can be mixed and matched to create a seemingly inexhaustible supply of route combinations. There is almost no end to the possibilities available to the adventurous mountain biker on the South Downs.

Off-road unicycling!

At 160km (100 miles), the South Downs Way National Trail (SDW) is the longest continuous long distance path (LDP) open to mountain bikers in the UK. The entire route can be traversed on bridleways and byways and involves some 3,800m (12,600ft) of ascent.

The ancient chalk downlands of the South Downs roll gently out from Winchester in the west, through the ancient pastures and woodlands of East Hampshire, across the forested estates, heathlands and Kipling's 'bow-headed, whale-backed' Sussex chalk hills, to the iconic cliffs of the Seven Sisters and Eastbourne in the east. The South Downs National Park contains two Areas of Outstanding Natural Beauty (AONBs) and constitutes one of the UK's best-known and most popular landscapes. The South Downs are located in the most densely populated area of the UK and record some 39 million visitor days every year.

The South Downs actually contain around 3200km of public rights of way, including the SDW. Many of these rights of way – including the SDW bridleway routes – are accessible to and very popular with horse riders and mountain bikers as well as walkers. At weekends, during school holidays and in the summer months in particular, the entire 160km length of the SDW and its subsidiary network of footpaths, bridleways and byways

The Channel coast from Cissbury Ring (Routes 13 and 14)

is alive with people enjoying the landscape on horseback and mountain bike as well as on foot.

Many of the Downs' bridleways and byways traverse chalk downland, which is well-drained and provides superlative off-road riding conditions for much of the year. However, the South Downs is a diverse landscape comprising many types of terrain, including woodland, pasture and heathland, which makes for a varied off-road experience, whether you're out for an hour or two, or all day.

When you're out on your bike among the rolling Downland scenery, it can feel like you're a very long way from the south east's densely populated urban landscape of towns, cities, motorways and shopping centres, but in reality you're never too far from civilisation and there are good transport links to the Downs from all over the south east (see below).

As well as assembling an exemplary collection of graded mountain biking routes with maps and route profiles, this guide includes extensive information on facilities and services available to mountain bikers, including pubs, cafés and water points along the routes as well as bike shops, accommodation and transport links. Biking-specific information on equipment and preparation is also included.

ABOUT THE ROUTES IN THIS GUIDE

The 160km South Downs Way National Trail is the centrepiece of the guide. Mountain bikers riding the SDW in its entirety approach the endeavour in a variety of ways. Some ride the route in stages at different times and others complete the whole route in one go. Of the latter, some will complete it over several days – camping or staying in accommodation along the way – while others will take two days and some seriously fit individuals ride the whole route in one day. Then there are those remarkable people who do what's known as the South Downs Double, which involves riding the whole route there and back – that's 320km (200 miles) – in 24 hours!

This guide breaks the SDW route down into three stages, with 'how to get there' information for each leg. These stages provide a good day's ride for mere mortals and can be combined into longer rides for the seriously fit.

Most people riding the SDW do so from west to east because of the prevailing winds – wind direction is an important factor for mountain bikers, especially when covering long distances and particularly on elevated and exposed terrain. It makes sense, therefore, to describe the route from west to east.

As with all the route descriptions in this guide, special attention is paid to the nature of the terrain encountered as well as the major climbs and descents involved and any particular hazards to be aware of. Facilities and services en route are also included.

The other routes in this guidebook are day, half-day and shorter routes around the Downs. They are distributed along the

length and breadth of the Downs, which are divided into five areas. The area sections are roughly analogous with the areas covered by the various Ordnance Survey Explorer maps covering the South Downs (see Maps below).

The routes are designed for maximum enjoyment of the mountain biking potential available on the South Downs, hence there is some overlap and repetition in the use of particular stretches of bridleway and byway between several of the routes. Roads are avoided wherever practical, although in many cases brief stretches of road here and there can link up some great off-road trails.

Trail centres

This guidebook does not include route descriptions for the mountain biking trail centres at the Queen Elizabeth Country Park on the Downs

One of several busy road crossings on the SDW (Route 15)

between Chichester and Petersfield, at Houghton Forest near Amberley and at Friston Forest near Seaford; nor informal trails such as those at Wild Park and Stanmer Park in Brighton. These dedicated trails are well worth visiting, especially for those with a fondness for singletrack and downhilling.

GETTING THERE AND GETTING AROUND

Essentially, there are three options for getting to the South Downs. Firstly, if you're lucky enough to live in this wonderful region you can always bike it. The second option is to travel by train. All the main centres along the South Downs are served by main-line routes from London and other parts of the south east. There are also good rail links between the main cities and towns around the Downs and the stations in between. Journey times from London take from less than an hour (52mins from London Victoria to Brighton) to an hour and a half (92mins from Victoria to Chichester). Connections to minor stations will obviously add to your journey time.

All of the rides in this guide either start from or are accessible from nearby railway stations. There are also options for extending or cutting short rides by means of other railway stations near the routes.

Most trains have dedicated space for two bikes, which is hardly adequate. Bikes can also go in the door areas, but this can be a hassle if you have to keep moving your bike to let people on and off. Engineering works often take place at weekends on the southern rail network, and rail replacement buses do not carry bikes – so check before travelling. There are rush hour restrictions on taking bikes on most lines in the south east, so check these out before making your journey. Timetable information, as well as information on engineering works and on bike restrictions, can be found at www.nationalrail.co.uk. Or call 08457 484950.

The third option is to travel by car. There are car parks at many sites all the way along the South Downs, which can make travelling by car easier and more convenient (car parks are indicated on the route maps). However, the less traffic there is around the National Park the better for everyone, so please leave your car at home unless using it is unavoidable because of time restrictions, engineering works or long-winded rail connections.

Andy Goldsworthy chalk ball (Route 11)

WHEN TO GO

The South Downs are superb for mountain biking all year round and each season has its own particular charms. Obviously downland bridleways and byways are at their driest in summer – when you can fairly zip along the ridges and enjoy greater traction on the uphills. But the summer months are also much busier than other seasons, especially at weekends and during the summer holidays, and so require greater vigilance for walkers, horse riders and other people out enjoying the Downs. Spring and autumn are that bit quieter, but the weather and therefore conditions on the ground are obviously less predictable.

Winter can be an excellent time for mountain biking on the Downs, as long as you're not frightened of getting muddy. However, after prolonged periods of rain the chalk/clay soil in certain areas can be transformed into a highly-adhesive quagmire, completely gumming up your bike and making riding impossible. This is no excuse to avoid the Downs in winter, as there are plenty of well-drained areas where mud isn't so much of a problem. Those areas prone to mud are indicated in the route descriptions.

SAFETY

Most of the time, mountain biking is a perfectly safe activity and arguably safer than riding on roads. However, rutted, slippery and loose surfaces are frequently encountered and if you

Watch out for adders basking on paths

take a tumble at speed, you risk causing considerable damage to yourself. Riding downhill at speed is one of the great joys of mountain biking, but it is essential that you maintain control. If you can't see who or what is coming round a bend, slow down. Likewise, if you have never ridden a particular downhill before and don't know what to anticipate, moderate your speed.

Make sure that your brakes are working efficiently and that your tyres are inflated properly (30–40psi depending on terrain, conditions, your weight and so on). Check that all quick releases are tight and wheels are secure.

Wear a helmet and appropriate clothing, carry a first aid kit, plenty of water, some high-energy snacks, a map, compass and a mobile phone. Wear some sunblock in summer. Carry waterproofs in wet weather. Carry spare inner tubes, a pump and basic tool kit. Carry lights if there's any chance that you'll be out after dusk (equipment is covered in more detail below). If you go riding on your own, let someone know where you're going and when you expect to return.

In case of injury or other incident, try to stay calm and assess your situation. If anyone with you is injured remember 'ABC' – airway, breathing, circulation (signs of life, blood loss). Make any casualties warm and comfortable and place any unconscious casualties in the recovery position. Try to ascertain your exact position on the map and consider your options for finding shelter, staying put or seeking help. Remember that it may take an emergency team some time to reach you. If you decide to call for help, call 999 and ask for both Police and Ambulance. Be ready to give the location of the incident (grid references, map sheet number, name of the area and description of the terrain), any injuries and names of casualties. Be prepared to supply the numbers of any phones carried by the party; describe the nature and time of the incident and weather conditions at the incident site, equipment at the site, including warm clothing and shelter, distinguishing features and markers at the site, and the location from which you are phoning if different from the incident site.

Equipment

Your bike

Out on the bridleways and byways of the South Downs you will encounter mountain bikers riding machines costing between a few hundred pounds and a few thousand. Your choice of bike is contingent on a number of factors but, generally, how much you spend depends on the relation between your disposable income and your degree of enthusiasm. There is no doubt that a top of the range, lightweight bike with high-specification components can only add to the enjoyment of off-road mountain biking. Better-made bikes also tend to perform more efficiently and, arguably, need less maintenance. However, when components need replacing they are also going to be more expensive.

There is little point spending thousands on a bike that only sees action a few times a year, but for those who are serious about their sport a good quality machine is essential. However, choosing the right type of mountain bike for you is a far more important business than the relative cost alone and it is best to seek the advice of industry professionals (see Appendix C) before buying.

Choosing the right frame size is a crucial factor, bearing in mind that a smaller frame than you would need for a road bike is better suited for off-road mountain biking. Front suspension forks are recommended for the often hard and bumpy flint-studded downland chalk tracks: but most mountain bikes come with front suspension forks as standard these days.

The South Downs are as appropriate terrain as any for full-suspension bikes, although many people prefer to ride 'hardtail' machines – that is, front

The steep climb from the Arun Valley (Route 12)

suspension only. This is a matter of personal preference dictated in part by the kind of riding you do.

Tools and maintenance

Whatever choices you make about the set-up of your bike, bear in mind that the more use it gets the more maintenance it will require. However expensive or inexpensive your bike, it needs to be looked after. By nature, mountain biking causes wear and tear, especially in wet and muddy conditions. It is important to keep your bike at least reasonably clean and keep its moving parts lubricated. A well-maintained bike performs better and its components will last longer.

In dry periods during the summer months, many paths on the South Downs develop a thick layer of fine chalk or earth dust. Combined with ordinary chain oil this dust produces a highly effective grinding paste that will punish your bike's drive-train. Using a 'dry' teflon chain lubricant reduces this phenomenon.

Learning the basics of bike maintenance and equipping yourself with elementary bike tools is a good idea. You should carry a small toolkit and pump with you while out riding and, at the very least, be able to repair a puncture, fix a broken chain and adjust your brakes and gears when necessary. A basic toolkit including a puncture repair kit, spare inner tube, tyre levers, allen key set, spoke key and chain link extractor can be carried in a saddle pack or backpack.

Negotiating the woodland track tree roots (Route 13)

Helmet

Most mountain bikers wear a helmet with very good reason. The nature of the activity means that taking a tumble is a likelihood at some point. If this occurs at speed you are at risk of serious injury. As well as injuries such as broken bones and serious gashes, a head injury can be fatal or cause permanent disability or paralysis. A helmet may not prevent such serious injuries in some cases, but in others it might.

First aid kit

Anecdotal evidence suggests that many mountain bikers don't carry a first aid kit with them. Granted that a first aid kit isn't much use if you break a collarbone – a not uncommon injury among mountain bikers – but there are plenty of occasions where a dressing and antiseptic wipes can be very useful. Downland

Climbing towards Bignor Hill (Route 12)

chalk is full of hard, sharp flints that can cause nasty gashes. All the more reason to wear a helmet. The accident and emergency departments of most Sussex and East Hampshire hospitals are no strangers to casualties with mountain biking related injuries: these are at Winchester, Chichester, Worthing, Brighton and Eastbourne.

Clothing

There is no shortage of biking-specific clothing on the market and specialised off-road gear comprises a significant part of this. With the funds and inclination hundreds of pounds can be spent on equipping yourself for mountain biking, and for the dedicated enthusiast this may be money well spent. However, there are some essentials worth considering even for infrequent off-roaders. Wickable base layers, underwear, mid-layers and top layers can make what is often a sweaty activity much more comfortable. Stopping for a breather in a sweat-drenched cotton top is asking for

trouble even in a light breeze. Shorts or wickable undershorts with a padded seat ensure a more comfortable relationship with your saddle, especially on longer rides.

Biking-specific waterproofs are designed for a close fit and freedom of movement so as to avoid drag or getting caught up in your bike's moving parts. Waterproofs should be a 'breathable' material – such as Gore-Tex.

Many mountain bikers use the SPD pedal system with shoes that clip on to the pedal using cleats, which provides greater stability and makes pedalling more efficient by engaging the 'backstroke'. Whether using SPDs, 'platform' pedals or other systems, waterproof overshoes or waterproof socks can be useful in wet conditions.

NAVIGATION

Many walkers and mountain bikers now use GPS (global positioning systems) for navigation: a number of biking-specific GPS are now on the market. GPS can make navigation easy and accurate and dispense with the need to carry maps. On the down side, they are not cheap and they are not infallible. For those without a GPS, a map and compass are just as useful for mountain bikers in unfamiliar territory as they are for walkers, although very few of the former seem to carry compasses. Although waymarking on the South Downs is extensive, it is still possible to lose your way – especially in wooded areas – and a compass can help prevent you heading miles off-course.

Hydration

There are a number of dedicated water points for walkers and mountain bikers to use at points along the SDW (see Appendix B), but always make sure you have plenty of water with you, especially during the summer and on longer rides. Many mountain bikers use hydration packs – a water reservoir, usually with one to two litre capacities, with a drinking tube usually carried in a purpose-designed, small backpack. Hydration packs allow you to carry more water than water bottles carried in frame-mounted bottle cages – which are more popular with road cyclists, and can easily be dislodged when riding off-road. Be sure to be adequately hydrated before setting off on your ride.

Biking-specific backpacks, which are designed to carry water reservoirs, come in various capacities and are usually designed to carry the essentials in internal pockets: tools, pump, waterproofs, snacks, mobile phone,

Poppy field above South Heighton (Route 24)

first aid kit, map and compass. They are also designed for a comfortable and stable fit for riding. If you are thinking about acquiring one, consider how much capacity you will need for the kind of riding you do.

Drinking water along the South Downs Way

There are few places where drinking water can be obtained along the South Downs Way. This is because much of the SDW runs along the crest of the Downs while villages and springs are found at the foot. Ensure that you carry enough water with you, especially in summer – when perhaps two litres per person per day may be required. See Appendix B for a comprehensive list of waterpoints.

FOOD

Carry enough food and/or make certain you can buy some en route. If your energy levels dip when riding it is difficult to maintain output on an empty tank. When walking, hunger can be ignored to a certain extent, but mountain bikers are prey to the phenomenon of gnawing pangs that won't go away, which is known in some parts as 'bonking'. It makes sense to carry lightweight, high-energy foods such as flapjacks, fruit cake, dried fruit and nuts, 'hi-energy' bars and bananas.

RIGHTS OF WAY AND OTHER USERS

Mountain bikers have 'right of way' on bridleways (indicated by blue

Chalk-hill blue butterfly

arrows on signposts and gates), on byways (red arrows) and on green lanes. This gives you the right to share the way with other users – always give way to walkers and horse riders. Don't approach walkers or horse riders at speed from behind or in front. When approaching from behind, slow right down and announce your presence with a 'hello' so as not to startle man or beast. When approaching from the front, slow down and give a wide berth or stop and make way for them to pass you.

Don't ride on footpaths: it's illegal, it can damage paths and sensitive heathland environments and it's really annoying for walkers. Besides, the bridleway and byway network on the Downs is so extensive that there's no need to use footpaths.

Waymarking

Waymarking on the South Downs is generally excellent, you will find waymarkers on gates and signposts at regular intervals and at path junctions – where you need them most.

Waymarking on the South Downs Way

As mentioned above, bridleways are indicated with blue arrows and in the case of the SDW those arrows incorporate the acorn emblem which indicates Long Distance Paths in England and Wales. Byways are indicated with red arrows and footpaths with yellow arrows, and these of course are out of bounds to mountain bikers and horse riders.

Although paths and tracks on the Downs are usually excellently maintained and comprehensively waymarked, it's still quite possible to get lost. Signposts are occasionally removed or damaged; routes can be changed temporarily or permanently for a variety of reasons and it's also quite easy at times to go whizzing past a path junction on your bike, oblivious to any waymarkers. There are also a few places where waymarkers are not obvious or clear; where this has been the case, or where there is a good chance of going astray for other reasons, it is noted in the route descriptions below.

The other situation where it's easy to get lost is when you are riding through managed woodland. Forestry plantations are often criss-crossed with tracks that are liable to be changed and therefore don't always correspond with the map. It can be quite easy to lose your bearings when all you can see are trees. Hence, as well as a carrying a map, a compass is extremely useful: it can save you going miles off course.

Maps

Ordnance Survey provides map coverage of the South Downs in 1:25,000 and 1:50,000 scales (see www. ordnancesurvey.co.uk/leisure).

The most up-to-date 1:50,000 scale Ordnance Survey mapping is used for the routes in this guidebook. At the time of going to press, the information on the maps included in this guide was accurate. A note of caution: the status of some rights of way may be changed over time. Most often – but not always – cyclists have been granted greater access rights with footpaths and other rights of way being 'upgraded' to permissive bridleways. Older copies of maps may contain information that is at odds with what is included here.

How to use this guide

Each of the three day stages of the SDW and the 23 other routes included in this guide are graded according to the degree of physical effort they require. The grades are:

- ■ medium
- ▲ hard
- ◆ very hard

OS 1:25,000 Explorer series

- 132 Winchester, New Alresford & East Meon – Routes 1 and 4–6
- 120 Chichester & the Downs, South Harting & Selsey – Routes 1, 2 and 7–11
- 121 Arundel & Pulborough, Worthing & Bognor Regis – Routes 2, 6 and 12–16
- 122 Brighton & Hove, Lewes & Burgess Hill – Routes 2, 3 and 16–22
- 123 Eastbourne & Beachy Head, Newhaven, Seaford, Hailsham & Heathfield – Routes 3, 21 and 23–26
- 133 Haslemere & Petersfield, Midhurst & Selbourne and 119 Meon Valley, Portsmouth, Gosport & Fareham – no specific route but cover surrounding areas

OS 1:50,000 Landranger series

- 185 Winchester & Basingstoke – Routes 1 and 4–6
- 197 Chichester & The South Downs – Routes 1, 2 and 7–16
- 198 Brighton & Lewes – Routes 2, 3 and 17–22
- 199 Eastbourne & Hastings – Routes 3, 21 and 23–26

Harvey Maps publish a lightweight, waterproof 1:40,000 single sheet map showing the whole of the SDW (see www.harveymaps.co.uk).

Digital Ordnance Survey mapping of the region is available from www.memory-map.co.uk and www.anquet.co.uk.

The grades reflect the length of the route, the number and severity of climbs and the nature of the terrain traversed. There is very little 'technical' mountain biking on the South Downs, hence there is no 'difficult' grade. The 'hard' and 'very hard' classifications in this guide focus on how strenuous the routes are. There are no 'easy' routes included here and, therefore, there is no 'easy' grade.

Distances are given in kilometres and metres throughout the route descriptions. The total distance given at the beginning of each route is given in kilometres with the equivalent in miles given in brackets. All distances given in metres are linear distances and not height gain unless specifically stated. 'Climb for 200m along the bridleway' means the climb is over a distance of 200m, as opposed to: '... ascend 200m as you climb along the bridleway for 500m'.

The total route distances are also broken down into off-road and on-road distances, with the off-road total given as a percentage. These off-road/on-road distances are as accurate as possible, allowing for a few grey areas where there is some uncertainty as to whether a particular section of a route really qualifies as a 'road' or not!

The route descriptions are detailed and map references are given where opportunities for uncertainty with route-finding occur. Once you have ridden the routes a couple of times they will become more familiar and you can spend less time with your nose in this book! Like following recipes from a cookery book, interpreting these routes in your own way and indulging in a spot of improvisation will adapt them to your own taste.

Although the routes in this guide incorporate the most up-to-date Ordnance Survey 1:50,000 mapping available at the time of publication, it is recommended that you also carry the relevant OS map sheets. You may also wish to carry a GPS as a further guide to navigation. Should you get lost or want to find railway stations, pubs, car parks or villages that are off the route, they will allow you to see the wider context.

Abbreviations and symbols used in the route descriptions

← left
→ right
↑ straight ahead
✗ path crossing/junction
N north
S south
E east
W west
NW etc. northwest etc.
LH and RH left-hand and right-hand

- Specific directions to readers are given as arrow symbols. Where the words **left** and **right** are in bold, they are not specific route directions to readers but as they describe the physical nature of roads, tracks or paths taken, they are still important for navigation. Where they are not in bold they relate to text that is not crucial to navigation – usually roads, tracks or paths that should not be taken. Where 'left-hand' and 'right-hand' are not abbreviated, they also relate, essentially, to incidental text. An example of how this is handled in the book is: '... ignore the first left-hand path. Continue ↑ as the path soon swings **left**...'

- Easy to miss paths to look out for when on routes are noted in **bold green**; warnings of steep, dangerous or possibly crowded routes in **bold red**.

- Place names in route descriptions that appear on their maps are noted in **bold**.

- Roads are shown as `A272`, motorways as `M3`.

- Grid references are shown as SU 478 300.

- Important signs along the way are noted in *red italics* in route descriptions.

Abbreviations
LDP – Long distance path
SDW – South Downs Way
MW – Monarch's Way
CW – Centurion Way
WSLT – West Sussex Literary Trail
KW – King's Way
PT – Pilgrim's Trail
IW – Itchen Way
WW – Weald Way
QECP – Queen Elizabeth Country Park

The South Downs Way National Trail
West to East – Winchester to Eastbourne

Climbing Bourne Hill (Day 3)

The South Downs Way: Introduction

The 160km (100-mile) SDW route is set out below in three day stages between 46.5km and 61km in length. These stages are intended as a guide that is very much open to adaptation – subject to your preferred way of tackling the route. You might want to take more or less time to complete the route; you might want to do it all in one go over the course of one, two, three or more days or you might prefer to complete stages at different times.

The length of stages you ride is contingent on several factors: your fitness; available time; the time of year, weather and ground conditions; transport links and where you choose to stay (see Appendix A for camping and accommodation). If attempting to complete the route in two days, Amberley is roughly halfway, has good train links, pubs and a campsite at nearby Houghton Farm. You will, however, have the tougher of the two days to come if riding west to east (there is no law against riding east to west, but you will be against the prevailing winds). Riding as far as Truleigh Hill YHA (101.5km) gets you well on the way, with a tough 56.5km to Eastbourne to tackle the following day. A four-day itinerary might be approximately: day 1: Winchester to Queen

The beech trees near Cheesefoot Head (Day 1)

Elizabeth Country Park (QECP) (next to the A3); day 2: QECP to Amberley; day 3: Amberley to Housedean Farm (on the A27 between Brighton and Lewes); day 4: Housedean Farm to Eastbourne.

There are plenty of pubs, quite a few cafés (listed at the beginning of route descriptions) and sufficient water points (see Appendix B) along or near the SDW. However, make sure you have plenty of water and high-energy snacks with you. Make sure also that you have adequate clothing, tools (including spare inner tubes, a pump and puncture repair kit), maps (or GPS) and a first aid kit. A mobile phone is invaluable in an emergency (see the equipment section above).

Route 1 South Downs Way:
Day One – Winchester to Cocking

START	Winchester train station SU 478 300 or opposite City Mill SU 486 293
FINISH	Cocking Hilltop car park SU 875 167
DISTANCE	56.5km (35 miles)
ON ROAD	16.75km (10½ miles)
OFF ROAD	39.75km (24½ miles)
VARIANT	61km (38 miles), via Old Winchester Hill
ON ROAD	16.75km (10½ miles)
OFF ROAD	44.25km (27½ miles)
ASCENT	1295m (4250ft); via Old Winchester Hill 1370m (4495ft)
GRADE	▲
TIME	4hrs 30mins–5hrs 30mins
PUB	Various in Winchester; The Bluebell at Cocking
CAFÉ	Various in Winchester; QECP café; Moonlight Cottage at Cocking

70% OFF ROAD

Overview

The terrain at the start of the South Downs Way (SDW), particularly between Winchester and the Meon Valley, is considerably gentler than the more hilly country encountered further east, easing the mountain biker in at the beginning of this long distance, off-road epic. This first day's route is marginally longer than the following day and arguably that bit easier. However, it should not be underestimated. Climbs include the steep (on-road) then steady (off-road) pull up from Chilcomb to Cheesefoot Head near the start; a tough, steep climb from Coombe Cross to Salt Hill; a long, steady ascent through Queen Elizabeth Country Park (QECP); a fairly steep, steady climb through woodland around Tower Hill and a steep ascent on chalk track to Phillisswood Down. The variant route includes Old Winchester Hill, which is a stop-start sort of climb and the final 200 metres are a killer. The route traverses some fine countryside, with great views south to the Solent and the Isle of Wight near the beginning, and north across the Low Weald, especially from Butser

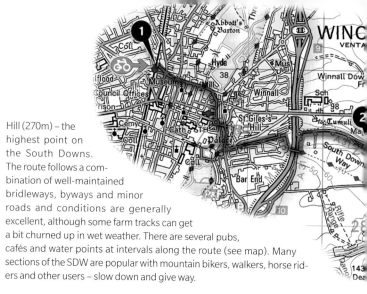

Hill (270m) – the highest point on the South Downs. The route follows a combination of well-maintained bridleways, byways and minor roads and conditions are generally excellent, although some farm tracks can get a bit churned up in wet weather. There are several pubs, cafés and water points at intervals along the route (see map). Many sections of the SDW are popular with mountain bikers, walkers, horse riders and other users – slow down and give way.

Directions

1 From Winchester train station head ↑ along Station Hill, keep ↑ over a mini-roundabout and take the third exit at the ✖ onto City Road. At the next ✖ continue ↑ onto North Walls (**B3330**). Continue to a fork, bearing → to continue on the **B3330** along Union Street. Union Street becomes Eastgate Street and continues to a roundabout. Keep ← onto High Street then turn → off the next mini-roundabout onto Chesil Street. Continue to a ✖ and turn ← onto East Hill (*SDW*). Climb to a fork, bear → and continue ↑ along Petersfield Road to join a path at the end of the road. Follow the path ↑ then turn → and continue round to a bridge over the **M3**. Once across, turn ← onto a path (*SDW*) running parallel to the **A31**. Follow the path to a roundabout, turn → and continue alongside the **A31**, before bearing → onto King's Lane.

The official SDW route start (marked in blue) is now open to cyclists. From the bridge over the River Itchen opposite the City Mill, head **south** (SDW) on to the riverside path. Follow this for 500 metres then on passing playing fields turn ← onto College walk. At a T-junction turn ← to stay on College Walk, which soon feeds ← into Wharf Hill. When you come to a crossroads at the **B3330**, cross ↑ into East Hill (SDW) and rejoin the main route.

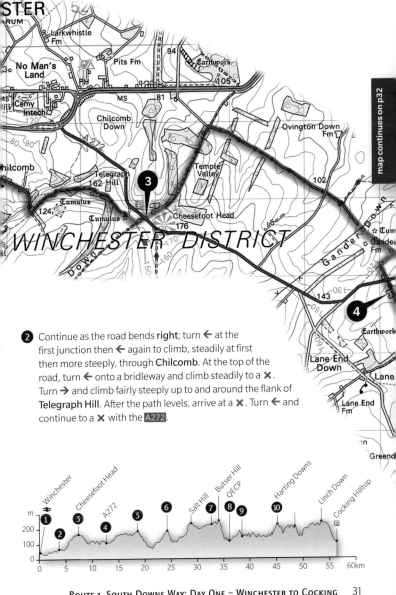

map continues on p32

WINCHESTER DISTRICT

2 Continue as the road bends **right**; turn ← at the
first junction then ← again to climb, steadily at first
then more steeply, through **Chilcomb**. At the top of the
road, turn ← onto a bridleway and climb steadily to a ✖.
Turn → and climb fairly steeply up to and around the flank of
Telegraph Hill. After the path levels, arrive at a ✖. Turn ← and
continue to a ✖ with the A272.

3 Cross over and continue ↑ along the SDW, passing through a stand of beech trees, soon descending steadily to pass some farm buildings and arrive at a ✕. Turn → to continue ↑ on the SDW, taking in a few minor ups and downs and passing through several gates and over several ✕s along the way. After descending a short way across **Gander Down**, pass through a gate and – forking ← – climb a little, passing through another gate. Continue along the field edge and, on approaching another gate, swing sharp → along the field edge instead (this is one of the easiest places to go astray on the whole SDW). Take the first ← through a gate (*SDW*) and continue to a road (A272).

4 Cross over and continue along a byway track through **Holden Farm**. Continue ↑ along tracks for 1.5km before emerging onto a country road. Continue ↑ for 1km, turn → at a ✕ then pass The Milburys pub and turn ← at a ✕. Continue along the road (the path runs parallel to the left-hand side of the road, but is best avoided if there are walkers) for 1km, then turn → off the road and go through a gate at **Wind Farm**; turn ← following signs for the *SDW*. Continue ↑ along a track to **Lomer Farm** then dogleg → then ← then → again to pass through the farmyard and exit along the SDW. Continue along a track before passing through a gate onto a country road. Turn → (↑) along a road and continue to a parking area by an area of woodland.

The SDW divides into three variants here – both bridleway routes are open to mountain bikers. The quicker, easier main route is described first: the longer, harder variant follows below.

5 At the parking area, turn first ← through a gate onto SDW/Monarch's Way bridleway variant. Descend through woods, pass through a gate and continue ↑ to descend along **Wheely Down**, passing through a couple more gates before turning → through a gate and then ← to descend on a track to Wheely Down Farm. Turn → onto a road and continue to a ✗ with the A32 at the **SW** edge of **Warnford**. Turn ← into the village then take the first **RH** turn off the A32 onto Old Winchester Hill Lane. Climb steadily along the lane for 2.75km before arriving at a gate just beyond a **LH** turn.

Variant via Exton and Old Winchester Hill

1 At the parking area, bear → along the road signposted for *Exton*. Turn sharp ← at the first junction and keep ← (↑) at the second. Descend steadily at first, becoming much steeper, along a narrow road known as The White

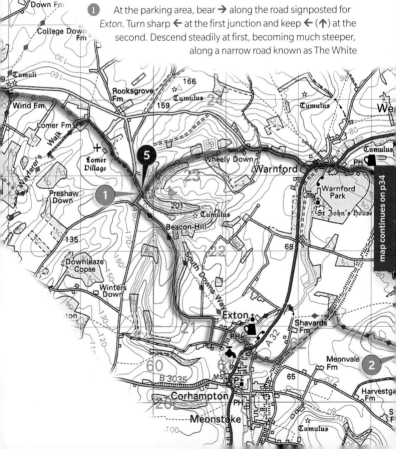

map continues on p34

Way. Shortly after the gradient eases, the road bends sharp **right**; continue to a ✕ with Allen's Farm Lane, turn ← then ← again after 200m and continue to a ✕. Turn → onto Beacon Hill Lane and follow this road through the village to the A32 (at time of writing there were signposts for the *temporary SDW route through Exton*). Cross ↑ over the A32 and continue along Stock's Lane for 500m, keep → at a fork then turn ← onto a bridleway (SDW) along a wooded dismantled railway line. Continue ↑ for 1km before turning → to drop off the dismantled railway line and

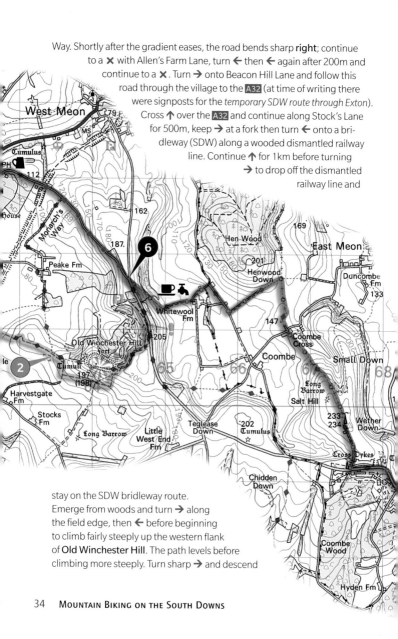

stay on the SDW bridleway route. Emerge from woods and turn → along the field edge, then ← before beginning to climb fairly steeply up the western flank of **Old Winchester Hill**. The path levels before climbing more steeply. Turn sharp → and descend a short way along a track then turn sharp ←. Continue ↑ for 700m before turning sharp ← and climbing very steeply for 200m.

② At the top of the climb, the path bears **right** and leads round to a gate near the summit of Old Winchester Hill. Go through and turn → along a bridleway track. Follow the track around to a gate by Old Winchester Hill Lane but don't go through. Instead, turn ← along the bridleway, which runs parallel to the road for 500m before it crosses over just before a car park and runs along the other side of the road. Arrive at a gate near a fork in the road.

• •

⑥ Go through the gate, descend a track across a very steep escarpment – **control your speed** – and pass through a gate at the bottom. Continue ↑ on a track to **Whitewool Farm**, turning ← past a large barn and continuing through the farm and past Meon Springs fishing ponds, before turning → along a farm road at a **✕**. After 500m, turn ← along a concrete track and soon begin climbing quite steeply to a ridge. At a **✕** turn → on a tree-lined track along the ridge. Cross ↑ over a road at **Coombe Cross** to continue on a bridleway and soon begin climbing very steeply along a path up **Salt Hill**, which

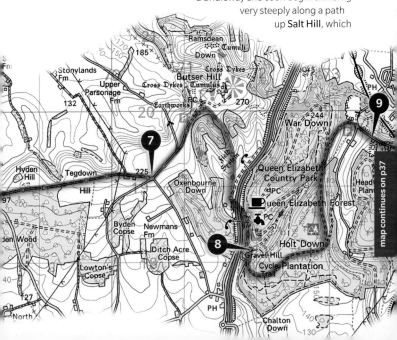

map continues on p37

is **very slippery when wet**. At the top, the path continues along a field edge and passes a radio mast before emerging onto Droxford Road. Turn ← and continue along the road. At a ✖ bear ← then keep ↑ over two more ✖s to continue along track. Continue ↑ and climb almost imperceptibly for over 2km before arriving at a ✖.

Approaching Butser Hill

7 Turn ← along the road and continue towards the car park near the summit of **Butser Hill**, before bearing → onto a bridleway (SDW) and arriving at a gate. Go through and follow the obvious track as it descends, gradually at first – becoming much steeper, along the grassy **S** flank of Butser Hill. Go through a gate halfway down and continue to descend the grassy slope before arriving at a gate along the field edge. Go through and up a slight rise; cross ↑ over two tracks – following signs for the *SDW* – and join a slip road to descend under the A3 road bridge.

Looking back to Butser Hill

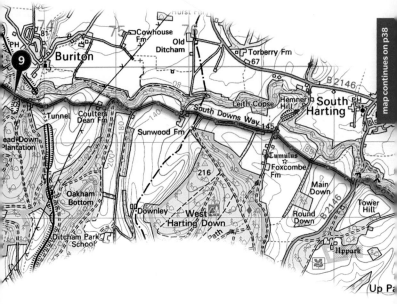
8 Continue ↑ into the QECP car park and pass around to the **right** of the visitor centre and café to continue ↑ along the road past parking and picnicking areas. Follow the road as it bends **left**, then take a → (SDW) then a ← and climb steeply through woodland. After the gradient eases keep ↑ at a ✘. The track levels then descends, steeply at first, then levels again – keep ↑ at a ✘ (SDW) – before descending steeply once more as it swings **E** and drops through the Kiln Lane car park. Exit the car park and continue ↑ over Kiln Lane and on to a minor road.

9 Continue along the winding narrow road with a little up and down, then climb through woods, continuing ← (↑) at a ✘ as the road emerges from the forest and descends a little towards **Sunwood Farm**. Pass the farm and, shortly after the road bends **left**, turn sharp → onto a broad bridleway track and climb steeply up to Hundred Acres. Continue ↑ along a broad track for the next 2km or so, losing and gaining a little height and passing ↑ over a ✘ onto Forty Acre Lane before arriving at the B2146. Cross the road to continue along bridleway, climbing steeply through woods to arrive at the B2141. Cross the road to rejoin the bridleway and climb steadily to **Harting Downs**.

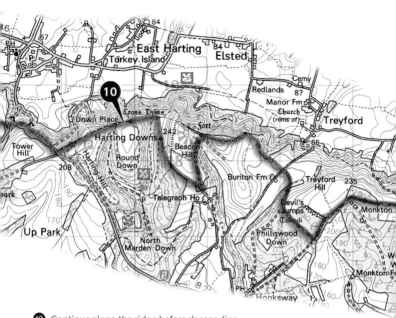

10 Continue along the ridge before descending
steeply along a chalk track to a gate. Go through and descend a
little further to a ✖. Turn ➜ with the SDW and climb steeply around the **W**
flank of **Beacon Hill**. At a ✖ turn ⬅ along the **E** flank of Beacon Hill, then
descend to a ✖ and continue ⬆ to climb steeply up and over Pen Hill.
Descend to the edge of woods, bear ➜ then keep ⬆ over a ✖ to continue
on the SDW. At the next ✖ (near **Buriton Farm**) dogleg ⬅ then ➜ and
soon begin climbing, steadily at first, becoming steeper, on chalk track.
Keep ⬅ at a fork shortly before the gradient eases then levels. At the next
✖ turn ⬅ and climb gently around the flank of **Treyford Hill**. As the SDW
bends **E**, continue ⬆ along the ridge, over **Didling Hill** and Linch Ball before
descending steeply over **Cocking Down** on chalk track that gives way to
farm road. Pass some livestock sheds before arriving at the A286.

A The nearest train station is Chichester, 14km to the south. By bike, the best option is to ride along the **A286** for 6km before joining the Centurion Way cycle route just south of West Dean for the remaining 8km.

The tough climb to Amberley Mount

Route 2 South Downs Way:
Day Two – Cocking to Ditchling Beacon

2

Start	Cocking Hilltop car park SU 875 167
Finish	Ditchling Beacon car park TQ 333 130
Distance	55.5km (34½ miles)
On road	4km (2½ miles)
Off road	51.5km (32 miles)
Ascent	1395m (4580ft)
Grade	▲
Time	4hrs 30mins–5hrs 30mins
Pub	The Bluebell at Cocking; The Plough at Pyecombe
Café	Moonlight Cottage at Cocking; Hiker's Rest at Saddlescombe Farm

95% OFF ROAD

Overview

This stage starts with a stiff climb up Manorfarm Down and then takes in five sections of the main South Downs ridge, which are variously intersected by the A285, the Arun Valley, the A24, the Adur Valley and the A23, before the final long, gradual climb to Ditchling Beacon. From the top of Manorfarm Down, the South Downs Way (SDW) traverses the ridge to Crown Tegleaze before descending precipitously to cross the A285, then climbing up and along the ridge to Bignor Hill and descending to the Arun Valley. After crossing the Arun, there is a long on-road then off-road climb to the summit of Amberley Mount; between Amberley Mount and Barnsfarm Hill, the SDW glides along the ridge on excellent tracks with a few minor ups and downs before the long descent to the A24. The very long, very tough climb from the A24 to Chanctonbury Ring is followed by a welcome coast along the ridge and then the descent to the Adur Valley. The long off-road, then on-road climb from the Adur to Truleigh Hill precedes a real rollercoaster ride along excellent chalk tracks taking in Edburton Hill, Perching Hill, Fulking Hill, Devil's Dyke and West Hill before dropping down to cross the A23 and beginning the stage's final climb to Ditchling Beacon. There are great views south and east across the Downs to the Channel coast and north across the Weald to the North Downs. The route follows a combination of well-maintained bridleways and

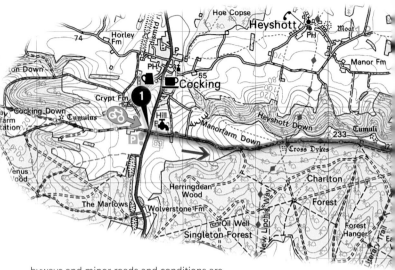

byways and minor roads and conditions are
generally excellent, although some tracks – especially those across the
valleys and declivities – can get a bit churned up in wet weather. There are many
pubs, several cafés and a few water points at intervals along the route (see map).
Many sections of the SDW are popular with mountain bikers, walkers, horse riders
and other users – slow down and give way.

Directions

1 From Hilltop car park, cross the road – **beware fast-moving traffic** – and
continue ↑ along Hillbarn Lane before beginning to climb steeply up
Manorfarm Down. When the gradient eventually eases, continue ↑ along

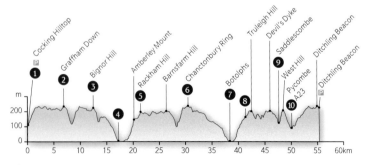

Passing Crown Tegleaze along Graffham Down

the ridge, gaining and losing a little height as the SDW gently
rolls along and enters woodlands. The track emerges from woods near
Graffham Down and continues gently rolling along before climbing a little
across the flank of Crown Tegleaze and entering woodland.

2 Emerge from the woods, go through a gate and descend **SE** (steadily at first becoming steeper) diagonally across fields along Littleton Down. Go through a gate and continue descending steeply to a **✗**. Descend **↑** on a farm road, passing **Littleton Farm** to arrive at the `A285`. Turn **→** onto the road then dogleg **←** onto a track road and continue **↑**. The track bends sharp **left** then **right** and begins to climb steeply, entering woods. The gradient eases then climbs steadily around the flank of Sutton Down. Continue **↑** over a **✗** and go through a gate and along a field edge on the flank of **Glatting Beacon**. Go through another gate, turn **←** then next **→** to continue **↑** past a parking area. Fork **→** onto a bridleway and soon begin to climb steadily up and over **Bignor Hill**.

3 Pass a memorial stone and descend steeply on a flinty chalk track. When the track bends **right**, **slow down**, turn sharp **←** at a **✗** and continue descending steeply. The track bends **right** near the bottom and arrives at a **✗** near some livestock sheds. Turn **→** then continue **↑** past the sheds and climb steadily before contouring along the hillside. Continue **↑** at the next **✗** and descend to the `A29`. Turn **→** along a track at the edge of the road for 100m, then cross the

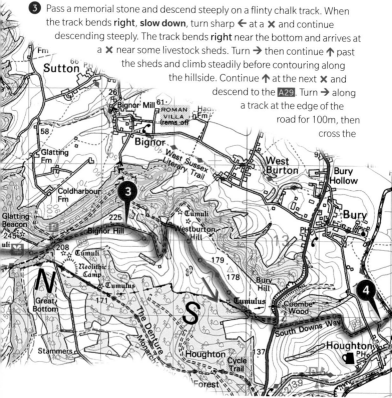

road to rejoin the bridleway and descend steeply along a chalk track. After 1 km, the track swings **right** then **left** and descends to Houghton Lane.

Stane Street Roman road near Bignor Hill

4 Cross the lane, go through a gate and continue across a field to another gate. Go through, turn → then ← and continue across a field to a further gate then bear → along the river bank. Continue around to the bridge, cross over, turn → then ← through a gate to leave the river bank. Continue along a track, which bends sharp **right** and crosses a bridge over a railway line to arrive at the B2139. Turn → on a track along the road edge to a crossing, cross over and continue on a track along the road edge, which turns **left** onto a minor road. Continue ↑ to climb steadily along High Titten road. Shortly after the

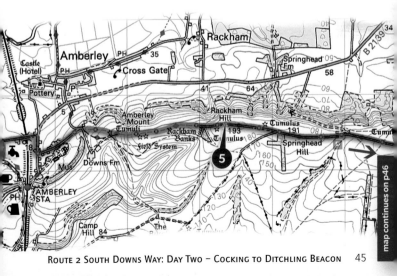

map continues on p46

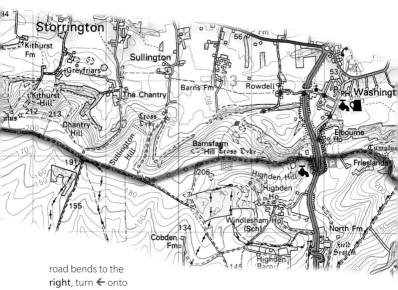

road bends to the
right, turn ← onto
a bridleway and climb a short sharp slope to a gate. Go through and
continue to climb before the track levels and arrives at a ✗. Continue ← (↑)
to climb very steeply up **Amberley Mount** on a rutted, grassy chalk track. At
the top, go through gates and continue along the ridge on a gradual incline
past **Rackham Banks** and **Rackham Hill**.

⑤ Continue ↑ along the ridge on a good track crossing **Springhead Hill**, then
lose and gain a little height over Kithurst Hill – **watch out for loose gravel on
the track** – and pass around two gates by Chantry Post car park. Continue
over **Sullington Hill**, go through a gate and fork ← to climb steadily over
Barnsfarm Hill before beginning the long descent across **Highden Hill**. The
track descends to a gate and then continues steeply down a lane, bending
sharp **right** at the bottom before arriving at the A24 . Turn ← along a path
next to the road and cross the northbound and southbound carriageways via
the central reservation at the obvious point. Cut ← across a grass bank on a
tarmac path and cross a slip road, bearing → onto a bridleway track, which
soon turns **right** into a car park. Begin climbing at length, steadily at first but
becoming much steeper, up a winding flint and chalk track. The track levels
and bends **left** at a ✗ to continue along the ridge, over a cattle grid and past
the wooded Iron Age hill fort of **Chanctonbury Ring**.

6 The track bends **SE**, descends a little to another cattle grid then descends along a broad, grassy flint track, continuing ↑ over a ✕. Continue ↑ along the ridge for another 2km before descending fairly steeply ↑ over another ✕ – **beware loose asphalt** – to arrive at a minor road. Turn → and cross the road then follow the bridleway next to the **LH** side of the road for 800m, keeping ↑ over a ✕. Turn ← through a gate and descend fairly steeply across a field on a narrow path, before climbing a little then passing through a gate to continue on a narrow path, which eventually

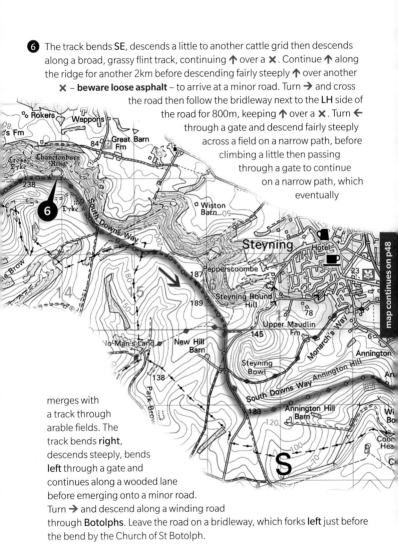

merges with a track through arable fields. The track bends **right**, descends steeply, bends **left** through a gate and continues along a wooded lane before emerging onto a minor road. Turn → and descend along a winding road through **Botolphs**. Leave the road on a bridleway, which forks **left** just before the bend by the Church of St Botolph.

map continues on p48

7 Continue to the river bank and follow it along to a bridge. Cross the bridge and continue ↑ before turning sharp ← after 200m to emerge at a layby on the **A283**. Continue along to the end of the layby and cross the road – **beware fast-moving traffic** – and turn ← along a path next to the road before turning → onto a bridleway. Climb very steeply on a narrow track, eventually arriving at a gate. Go through and continue climbing gradually across a field around the flank of **Beeding Hill**. Go through a gate and continue across a small parking area to a ✖.

8 Turn ← onto a minor road and climb steadily along the ridge to **Truleigh Hill**. The road gives way to a rutted track and passes the YHA, houses, a farm and the communications masts at the top of Truleigh Hill, before descending steeply on a chalk track to a ✖ on a saddle. Continue ↑ through a gate and climb steeply around Edburton Hill before descending steeply again to another saddle. Go through a gate and climb steeply up and over **Perching Hill**, then **Fulking Hill**.

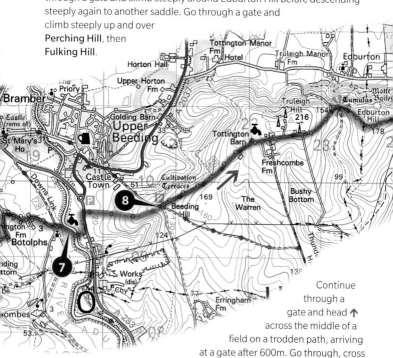

Continue through a gate and head ↑ across the middle of a field on a trodden path, arriving at a gate after 600m. Go through, cross Devil's Dyke Road, go through another gate and continue on a slight descent along Summer Down. After 1km, the descent becomes ever steeper – **watch out for walkers and horse riders** – and bends sharply **left** before passing through a gate and levelling out to cross a road.

9 Go through a gate, up a rise and turn **→** to continue **↑** along a track road through farm

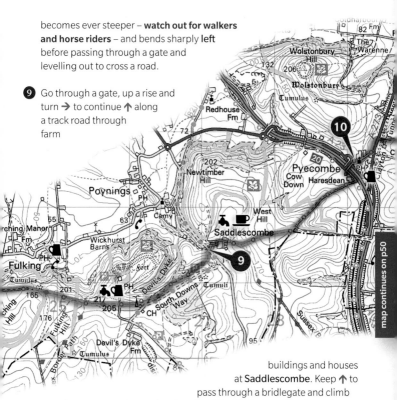

buildings and houses at **Saddlescombe**. Keep **↑** to pass through a bridlegate and climb along a steepening sunken lane for 200m, before passing through a gate. Continue **↑** and follow a fence up a steep grass slope for 400m, then pass through a gate to the **S** of **West Hill**'s summit (211m). Continue **↑** on a gradual descent, which soon steepens, and descend a broad, rutted chalk track – **control your speed**. Pass through a gate near the bottom and continue **↑** onto a farm road at **Haresdean**, which swings **left** onto a slip road, and then turn **→** at the next **✗** to cross the A23 on a road bridge.

10 Once across, turn **→** off the slip road and climb past a church on a narrow lane. Keep **↑** at a **✗** and descend to the A273. Turn **←** and follow a path alongside the road for 200m. Cross the road and continue past **Pyecombe golf course** to join a bridleway. Continue **↑** for 1km then turn

The South Downs near Ditchling Beacon

sharp ← and continue for 400m through New Barn Farm to a ✖. Turn → and continue along the ridge (with some up and down), passing through several gates before arriving at **Ditchling Beacon** (248m) after 3km.

The nearest train stations are Ⓐ Hassocks (5km) on the London–Brighton line, Ⓑ Falmer (7km) on the Brighton–Lewes line and Ⓒ Brighton (9.5km). To get to Hassocks, descend steeply **NW** on the Ditchling Road, continue to Ditchling then turn ← along the B2116 to Hassocks. For Falmer, descend **SW** along Ditchling Road to a ✖ then turn ← over the brow of the hill, descend under a road bridge along Coldean Lane to a ✖ with the A27, then follow a cycle path **ENE** to Falmer. For Brighton, descend **SW** along Ditchling Road to a ✖ and dogleg ← then → over a road bridge to continue along Ditchling Road, climbing past a golf course, then descending at length to the town centre and train station.

Pedalling along the gently rolling Kingston Ridge

Route 3 South Downs Way:
Day Three – Ditchling Beacon to Eastbourne

3

START	Ditchling Beacon car park TQ 333 130
FINISH	Eastbourne train station TV 609 991
DISTANCE	46.5km (29 miles)
ON ROAD	7.25km (4½ miles)
OFF ROAD	39.25km (24½ miles)
ASCENT	1020m (3345ft)
GRADE	▲
TIME	3hrs 30mins–4hrs 30 mins
PUB	The Abergavenny Arms at Rodmell; numerous in Eastbourne
CAFÉ	A couple in Alfriston (and a shop in the post office); numerous in Eastbourne

85% OFF ROAD

Overview

This is the shortest of the three stages of the South Downs Way (SDW) National Trail route described in this guide, but it is far from an easy ride – especially when you already have the previous 112km of the Long Distance Path in your legs. There are five major climbs: a steep, difficult climb through woodland at Bunkershill Plantation; a short, sharp then long, steady pull up to Newmarket Hill; a long, steep, curving climb up Itford Hill on chalk track and grass slope; and a long climb from the Cuckmere Valley to the summit of Windover Hill, initially on a steep, often slippery tree-lined track before a long haul up one of the finest chalk tracks on the South Downs. The final climb from Jevington to the top of Bourne Hill is long, but not too tough. This is a challenging route by any standards, but it is also a glorious ride on varied terrain, including woodland tracks and downland ridges. There are fine views of the English Channel, the Pevensey Levels and across the Sussex Weald to the North Downs to be enjoyed along the way. Two minor variants, at Alfriston and near Jevington, avoid awkward 'bottleneck' areas that can snarl you up with walkers and horse riders. There are several pubs, cafés and water points at intervals along the route (see map). The route is mostly on well-maintained bridleways, although there are several short road sections. Conditions are generally good but some farm tracks can get a bit churned up in wet weather. Many sections of the SDW are popular with other users – slow down and give way.

Directions

1 From the car park cross the road, go through a gate and continue **E** along the gently-undulating ridge for 2km, gaining and losing a little height a couple of times. Descend to a gate, pass through and cross a farm road **N** of **Streathill Farm** before climbing a little to **Plumpton Plain** on a broad chalk track. Continue along the level track for 1km before descending to a gate and a ✗ but don't go through. Turn ➔ to continue on a slight descent for 1km to a ✗. Turn ← and go through a gate; descend for nearly 2km, passing through two gates to arrive at a ✗. Turn ➔ through a gate and descend a path **pot-holed by rabbit burrows**. This bottoms out then begins to climb in an inverted S-curve through **Bunkershill Plantation**. This is a short, tough climb, which is **slippery after rain**. Continue through woods, emerging on the brow of Long Hill.

2 Descend the steep hillside with care, slowing before reaching the gate at the bottom. Pass through, descend several steps, turn ➔ onto a cycle path and follow it past **Housedean Farm** before

Descending from Plumpton Plain

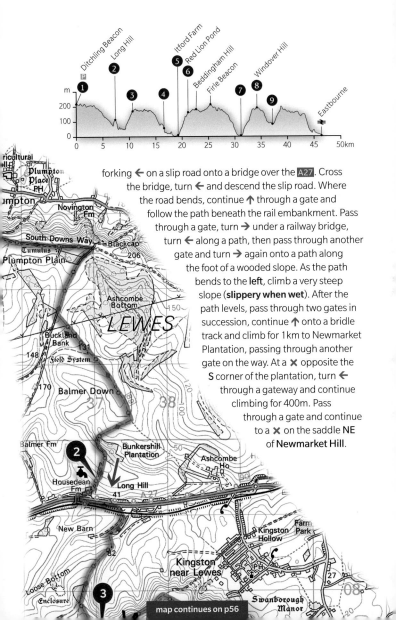

forking ← on a slip road onto a bridge over the **A27**. Cross the bridge, turn ← and descend the slip road. Where the road bends, continue ↑ through a gate and follow the path beneath the rail embankment. Pass through a gate, turn → under a railway bridge, turn ← along a path, then pass through another gate and turn → again onto a path along the foot of a wooded slope. As the path bends to the **left**, climb a very steep slope (**slippery when wet**). After the path levels, pass through two gates in succession, continue ↑ onto a bridle track and climb for 1km to Newmarket Plantation, passing through another gate on the way. At a ✗ opposite the **S** corner of the plantation, turn ← through a gateway and continue climbing for 400m. Pass through a gate and continue to a ✗ on the saddle **NE** of **Newmarket Hill**.

map continues on p56

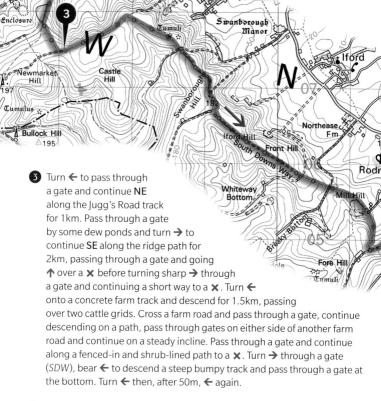

3 Turn ← to pass through a gate and continue **NE** along the Jugg's Road track for 1km. Pass through a gate by some dew ponds and turn → to continue **SE** along the ridge path for 2km, passing through a gate and going ↑ over a **✖** before turning sharp → through a gate and continuing a short way to a **✖**. Turn ← onto a concrete farm track and descend for 1.5km, passing over two cattle grids. Cross a farm road and pass through a gate, continue descending on a path, pass through gates on either side of another farm road and continue on a steady incline. Pass through a gate and continue along a fenced-in and shrub-lined path to a **✖**. Turn → through a gate (*SDW*), bear ← to descend a steep bumpy track and pass through a gate at the bottom. Turn ← then, after 50m, ← again.

4 Continue **NE** for 1km along a track (**prone to mud**) then turn → before the track reaches the **C7** road. Climb a little, pass through a gate and climb steeply a short way before descending through a gate to a road **✖**. Dogleg → then turn ← down through **Southease** on a country road across the Ouse Valley, then cross a bridge over the River Ouse. Continue ↑ and turn ← then → to pass through gates over a railway level crossing – **make sure the level crossing lights indicate that it is safe to cross**.

5 Continue towards **Itford Farm**, turn → (*SDW*) and follow the path across a bridge over the **A26**. Turn → at a **✖** and begin the long, winding climb up **Itford Hill**. The path initially climbs steeply **E**, then bends **S** and passes through a gate: the gradient eases then steepens once more as the path bends **E** again. Turn ← at a **✖** and climb **NE** on an ever-steepening grassy slope. The path bends **E** again near the top of the ridge. Continue on the

The arable fields beneath Mill Hill near Southease

map continues on p58

as the path trends **NE**, climbing a little and passing through a gate before reaching the summit trig point (164m) by **Red Lion Pond**.

6 Continue ↑ to a ✖ before reaching the communications towers on **Beddingham Hill**. Cross a cattle grid and continue ↑ past the towers before descending steadily and passing through a gate after 1km. Cross a farm road and continue ↑ through a car park, exiting through a gate on the **left**. Continue along the ridge on the SDW, climbing gently for 1.5km before passing over **Firle Beacon** (217m). Continue **SE**, drop down through a gate to pass Bopeep car park after 1km, pass through gates and climb over

Bostal Hill. Continue SE for 1km, ↑ over a ✖ and through a gate, before beginning the 2.5km descent to Alfriston. Pass through two gates and over a ✖ after 1km, soon swinging **S** and descending steeply on a broad chalky track (**can be very slippery in the wet**) that becomes a residential street as it enters **Alfriston.** Follow the street to a ✖ and take the second → to arrive on Alfriston Road after 50m. Turn ← then continue ↑ (leaving the SDW) and take the **RH** fork past the old market cross to head **N** out of the village. After 500m, turn → at a ✖ then continue ↑ to cross the Cuckmere River on Long Bridge.

Following the SDW through Alfriston is a hassle as you have to dismount to cross the footbridge over the Cuckmere River and this section of path is often very busy with walkers and horse riders.

7 At a ✖ where the road bends, continue ↑ to rejoin the SDW on a tree-lined track. Climb on a steep, tricky path to a country road next to a car park. Cross the road, pass through a gate and continue ↑. The climb is gradual at first, then more steep on a chalk and flint track that curves around the flank of **Windover Hill** before sweeping around once more to cross the summit (188m) after 1.5km.

8 Continue ↑ and pass through a gate, then turn → to head **SE** along the ridge on the SDW. Keep ← at a fork and continue for 1.5km as the path bends **S** and **SE** again, passing through two gates along Holt Brow. After the second gate, continue ↑ for 150m to a ✗. Turn ← and descend steeply through woodland – **watch out for walkers and horse riders**. After 300m, take the **RH** fork at a ✗ and continue ↑ over a second ✗ shortly after. Descend a narrow track, which is hemmed in by trees on one side and a stock fence on the other, taking care over exposed tree roots and watching out for walkers and horse riders – **control your speed**. Descend past St Andrew's church, where the track gives way to tarmac, shortly arriving at a ✗ with Jevington Road. Turn → then take the second **LH** turn onto the SDW on a bridleway.

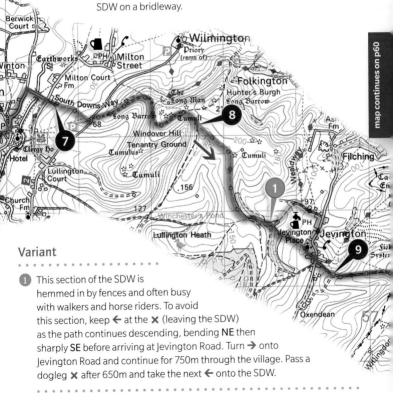

map continues on p60

Variant

1 This section of the SDW is hemmed in by fences and often busy with walkers and horse riders. To avoid this section, keep ← at the ✗ (leaving the SDW) as the path continues descending, bending **NE** then sharply **SE** before arriving at Jevington Road. Turn → onto Jevington Road and continue for 750m through the village. Pass a dogleg ✗ after 650m and take the next ← onto the SDW.

9 Begin the long, steady climb up the western spur of Bourne Hill, crossing the summit (201m) after 1.5km. Continue **SE** along the ridge on the SDW looking down on Eastbourne to the **E**. Cross the `A259` after 2.5km, then continue ↑ before taking the **RH** fork after 400m. At a ✕ keep ↑ then bear ← (*SDW*) to follow the path along the edge of woods. Cross ↑ over the `B2103` (*SDW*) and continue without losing height. At a second ✕ (*SDW*) turn ← and descend – keeping ← at a fork. The path swings **right** before emerging onto the `B2103` by the Kiosk café. Continue ↑ (→) for 100m then turn ← onto Holywell Road. Keep ↑ along Meads Street for 500m and turn → onto Meads Road at a mini-roundabout. Keep ↑ over the Meads Roundabout and continue along Meads Road for 1km. Continue ↑ onto South Street then bear ← onto Gildredge Road (`A259`) and continue ↑ to the **station**.

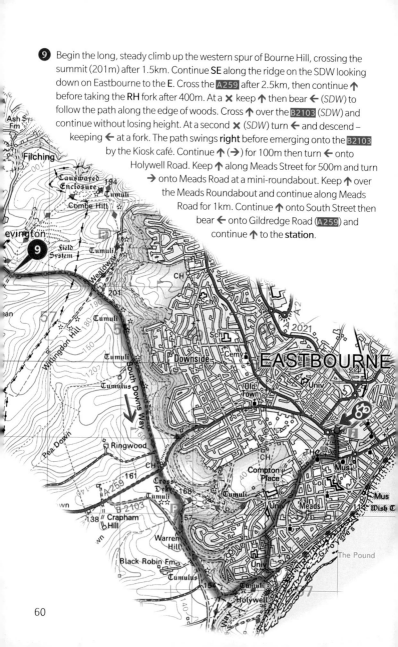

Beginning the long, tricky descent of Limekiln Lane (Route 6)

Routes around Winchester

Approaching Wheely Down along the Monarch's Way

Route 4
New Alresford – Warnford Circuit

START/FINISH	Watercress Line scenic railway car park, New Alresford SU 589 325 (parking available)
DISTANCE	29km (18 miles)
ON ROAD	10.5km (6½ miles)
OFF ROAD	18.5km (11½ miles)
ASCENT	450m (1475ft)
GRADE	■
TIME	2hrs–2hrs 30 mins
PUB	Several in New Alresford
CAFÉ	Station Café at New Alresford

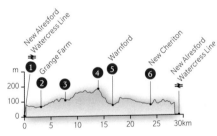

65% OFF ROAD

Overview
This is perhaps the least hilly of all the routes in this guide, starting and finishing in New Alresford and taking in the swathe of gently rolling down-land east of Winchester. As well as sections of the South Downs Way (SDW), the Monarch's Way (MW) and the Itchen Way (IW), this route also follows a number of restricted byways, several of which have no signposts or waymarks. With the exception of a fairly stiff climb near the beginning of Bosenhill Lane, there are no noteworthy climbs on this route. As well as the Long Distance Paths (LDPs), the other bridleways and byways on the route are popular with horse riders, dog walkers and other users. Sections of the route are particularly prone to mud after wet weather – especially between Warnford and New Alresford – so this is best considered as a summer or early-autumn ride.

This route can be combined with Route 5, to make a 59.5km ride with 955m ascent, taking 4hrs 30mins–5hrs 30mins (see Route 5 for details).

Directions

1 From the station car park, follow the exit road to join the `B3046`, turning ← to head **S** and passing through a tunnel under the railway line. Follow the `B3046` for 1.3km until it leaves town. Immediately after you have crossed the `A31` on the `B3046` road bridge, turn → off the road onto a bridleway. Continue ↑ as the path runs parallel to the `A31`, and ignore the first left-hand path. Continue ↑ as the path soon swings **left** away from the `A31`, becoming more of a track running between arable fields. The track soon passes through Vernal Farm before reaching a road. Turn ← and follow the narrow road around to **Tichborne**. Pass through the village as the road bends sharp **left** then sharp **left** again shortly after. At the second bend, turn sharp → off the road onto a bridleway at **Grange Farm**.

2 Continue ↑ on a good track, gaining height gradually over the course of 2km. Where the bridleway forks, keep →. The track soon bends **right** then **left** shortly after. Continue ↑ to a ✗ near a large hay shed, then turn ← onto the SDW.

This is where those combining this route with Route 5 join the trail.

Descend a short way across **Gander Down**, pass through a gate and – forking ← – climb a little, passing through another gate. Continue along the field edge and on approaching another gate, swing sharp → along the field edge instead (**this is one of the easiest places to go astray on the whole SDW**). Take the first ← through a gate (*SDW*) and continue to the `A272`.

3 Cross over and continue along a byway track through **Holden Farm**. Continue ↑ along tracks for 1.5km before emerging onto a country road. Continue ↑ for a further 1km, turn → at a ✗ to pass The Milburys pub and turn ← at a ✗. Continue along the road (a path runs parallel to the left-hand side of the road, but is best avoided if there are walkers) for 1km, then turn → off the road and go through a gate at **Wind Farm**, following signs for the *SDW*. Continue ↑ along a track to **Lomer Farm**, then dogleg → then ← then → again to pass through the farmyard and exit along the SDW. Continue along a track before passing through a gate onto a country road. Bear → (↑) along the road and, on arriving at a parking area next to an area of woodland, turn ← through the gate onto the MW and the SDW bridleway variant.

4 Descend through woods, pass through a gate and continue ↑ to descend along **Wheely Down**. Pass through a couple more gates before turning → through a gate and then ← to descend along a track to Wheely Down Farm. Turn → onto a road and continue to a ✕ with the `A32` at the **SW** edge of **Warnford**. Turn ← along the road into the village then take the first **LH** turn off the `A32`.

This route follows a number of wooded byways

5 Follow the narrow road as it winds past houses and farm buildings, then turn ← onto a byway track at College Farm. There is **no signpost**, but a sign by the house next to the track indicates *The Old Calfshed*. Continue along a tree-lined track, which is **prone to mud** after wet weather, and soon encounter a fairly stiff climb along Bosenhill Lane. The track then levels and descends before arriving at a ✕. Turn ← and continue to a road. Dogleg ← and look out for an **unsignposted** byway on the **RH** side of the road. Follow this track through woods, which gives way to concrete farm road before emerging from trees and continuing along the woodland edge. Arrive at a ✕ by New Pond Cottages and turn ← onto a restricted byway. Continue ↑ then cross ↑ over a small road and continue until the track emerges onto a road. Turn sharp → and continue into **New Cheriton**.

6 Cross ↑ over the `A272` and continue a short way along the `B3046`, turning → off the road onto a lane to join the IW. The narrow lane climbs a little past some houses before emerging into fields and becoming wider. Continue ↑ on the IW along Hinton Lane for the next 2.5km, crossing several tracks and a minor road and gaining and losing a little height along the way before emerging onto the `B3046`. Turn → onto the road and continue ↑ back into New Alresford.

On the SDW near Gander Down

Route 5

Winchester – Gander Down Circuit

START/FINISH	Winchester train station SU 478 300
DISTANCE	30.5km (19 miles)
ON ROAD	10.5km (6½ miles)
OFF ROAD	20km (12½ miles)
ASCENT	505m (1660ft)
GRADE	▲
TIME	2hrs 30mins–3hrs
PUB	Various in Winchester
CAFÉ	Various in Winchester

Overview

The countryside at the start of the South Downs Way (SDW), between Winchester and the Meon Valley, is gentler than the hillier landscapes encountered further east. This route takes to the

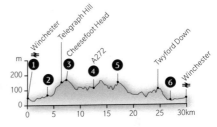

gently-gradiented Downland immediately east of Winchester and includes sections of the SDW, the Pilgrim's Trail (PT) and King's Way (KW) LDPs. The only real climbs are the steep (on-road) then steady (off-road) pull up from Chilcomb along the SDW to Cheesefoot Head and the short, sharp climb from Oakclose Plantation to Longwood Warren. Once above Winchester, there are good views south to The Solent and the Isle of Wight.

This route follows the start of Route 1 SDW Day One to the SDW/A272 ✗ at SU 561 269. To extend this ride by 2hrs–2hrs 30mins, you can join the circular Route 4 just before this point (at SU 554 279, start at point ❸ in the Route 4 description above) and follow it back to this point before continuing along Route 5. This makes for a total ride of 55km, 4hrs 30mins – 5hrs 30mins.

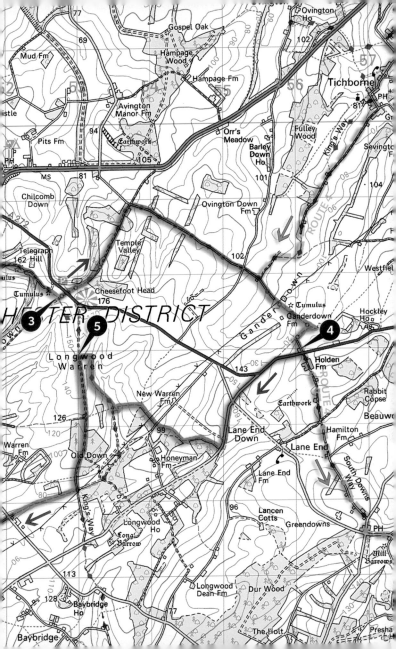

Directions

1 From Winchester train station head ↑ along Station Hill, keep ↑ over a mini-roundabout and take the third exit at the City Road. At the next ✖ continue ↑ onto North Walls (**B3330**). Continue to a fork, bearing → to continue on the **B3330** along Union Street. Union Street becomes Eastgate Street and continues to a roundabout. Keep ← onto High Street then turn → off the next mini-roundabout onto Chesil Street. Continue to a ✖ and turn ← onto East Hill (*SDW*). Climb to a fork, bear → and continue ↑ along Petersfield Road to join a path at the end of the road. Follow the path ↑ then turn → and continue round to a bridge over the **M3**. Once across, turn ← onto a path (*SDW*) running parallel to the **A31**. Follow the path to a roundabout, turn → and continue alongside the **A31**, before bearing → onto King's Lane.

2 Continue as the road bends **right**; turn ← at the first junction then ← again to climb, steadily at first then more steeply, through **Chilcomb**. At the top of the road, turn ← onto a bridleway and climb steadily to a ✖. Turn → and climb fairly steeply up to and around the flank of **Telegraph Hill**. After the path levels, arrive at a ✖ and turn ← to continue to a ✖ with the **A272**.

3 Cross over and continue ↑ along the SDW, passing through a stand of beech trees, soon descending steadily to pass some farm buildings and arrive at a ✖. Turn → to continue ↑ on the SDW, taking in a few minor ups and downs and passing through several gates and over several ✖s along the way. After descending a short way across **Gander Down**, pass through a gate and – forking ← – climb a little, passing through another gate. Continue along the field edge and, on approaching another gate, swing sharp → along the field edge instead (this is one of the easiest places to go astray on the whole SDW). Take the first ← through a gate (*SDW*) and continue to a road (**A272**).

4 Turn → along the **A272** for 700m before turning first ← (↑) onto a smaller road. Continue ↑ over a ✖ at **Lane End Down** (*Owlesbury and Upham*) and descend steadily along the road for 600m, turning → onto a bridleway just before the road enters some woods. Descend along the track then level out and continue along the edge of woods before descending again to a ✖. Continue ↑ and climb to a ✖ by a tanker; bear ← and descend steeply to a ✖. Bear → and climb steeply along a narrow track, which **can be overgrown in summer**. Continue to a ✖ and go ↑ to climb along the edge of woods. The track turns sharp **left** then arrives at a ✖.

5 Turn ← and descend steadily along the KW, continue ↑ over a ✖ and enter woods, keeping → (↑) at a fork to arrive at a ✖ after 1.8km. Turn → along the bridleway track, continuing ↑ over a road ✖ after 1km. Continue along

Riding through the woods along Old Down

the Stag's Lane track and emerge onto a minor road near some farm sheds; dogleg → then ← and continue along a narrow lane, keeping → (↑) at a fork. Continue to a ✖ and turn → (joining the PT) to descend along Mare's Lane to a ✖. Dogleg → then ← to continue ↑ along the bridleway, which becomes a wooded lane. At the next ✖ jink ← then → to continue ↑ on a rolling route across Hazeley Down and **Twyford Down**. Go through a gate, bear ← and continue to and through another gate. Turn ← to cross a bridge over the M3 and go through a gate on the opposite side. Descend fairly steeply, bear ← as the gradient eases and continue along the valley to a gate at the **SW** foot of **St Catherine's Hill**.

6 Go through and turn ← onto a tarmac track for 600m, then turn → at a ✖. Pass round a gate and continue along Five Bridges Road, which leads across the River Itchen. Turn → onto St. Cross Road and continue **N** for 2.3km to a ✖. Turn → onto High Street then next ← onto Jewry Street. Continue to a ✖ and turn ← onto City Road; continue ↑ to the train station.

Beneath St Catherine's Hill, Winchester

The final, strenuous climb to Old Winchester Hill

Route 6

Winchester to Petersfield (and return variants)

6

START	Winchester train station SU 478 300
FINISH	Petersfield train station SU 743 235
DISTANCE	52km (32½ miles)
ON ROAD	19km (12 miles)
OFF ROAD	33km (20½ miles)
SHORT RETURN ROUTE	58.5km (36½ miles)
ON ROAD	24km (15 miles)
OFF ROAD	34.5km (21½ miles)
LONG RETURN ROUTE	79.5km (49½ miles)
ON ROAD	30km (18½ miles)
OFF ROAD	49.5km (31 miles)
ASCENT	890m (2930ft); short return 1025m (3365ft); long return 1395m (4575ft)
GRADE	▲ (return routes are ◆)
TIME	4–4hrs 30 mins; short return 4hrs 30mins–5hrs; long return 6hrs–6hrs 30 mins
PUB	Various in both Winchester and Petersfield
CAFÉ	Various in both Winchester and Petersfield

65%
OFF ROAD

Overview

This route comes with three variants, which are contingent on your available resources of time and energy. The linear route takes you east along the Downs as far as Butser Hill before dropping off to Petersfield. The circular variants come in two sizes: the shorter is tough, the longer is very tough and an option only for the very fit. It is too big a ride for winter or wet conditions. The various permutations of this route take in much of the East Hampshire Downs, which is a generally gentler landscape than the rolling Sussex Downs. However, this route manages to take in a

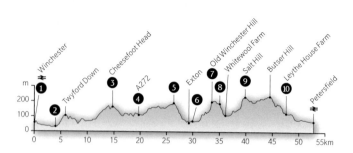

number of tough climbs and some exciting descents. If you're up to the challenge of the longer return route, you may need to take advantage of the various pubs and cafés en route. The routes follow sections of the South Downs Way (SDW) and Monarch's Way (MW) for much of the way, but there are also plenty of off-LDP bridleways and byways, which combine to make this an excellent ride or three.

Directions

1 From the station entrance, turn → along Station Road then bear ← onto Gladstone Street. Fork → onto Sussex Street and follow it round to High Street. Keep ← at the roundabout by West Gate, continue to a fork, dismount and continue → down the High Street (one-way on this section) to a bronze equestrian statue. Turn → along Trafalgar Street then ← along St Clement Street to a ✗. Turn → onto Southgate Street and continue S (becomes St Cross Road) for 2km. Turn ← onto Five Bridges Road, which leads across the River Itchen. Pass around a gate to arrive at a ✗ and turn ← along a tarmacked bridleway for 600m before turning → through a gate at the SW foot of **St Catherine's Hill**.

2 Continue ↑ to climb gradually up through the valley before bearing → and climbing more steeply to arrive at a gate. Go through and cross a bridge over the M3 motorway. Once across, turn immediately → through a gate and join the Pilgrim's Trail (PT) LDP. Go through a gate and continue ↑ along the bridleway across **Twyford Down**. **The track is narrow in sections** and down-and-ups a couple of times. Continue ↑ over the first ✗ then dogleg ← and immediately → at the second ✗ to continue ↑ along an initially wooded path before arriving at a road ✗. Continue ↑ along a narrow lane for 1km, climbing steadily. Take the first **LH** turn along a very narrow, winding road for almost 1km before arriving at a ✗. Dogleg → then ← to continue ↑ along the Stag's Lane track. Cross over a road ✗ to follow a bridleway into woods. At the next ✗ turn ← and begin a very long, steady climb up towards

Cheesefoot Head.
Just before arriving at the `A272`, turn sharp ← opposite a tanker and drop a short distance along a field edge before turning sharp → and climbing a little to a ✖. Turn → to join the SDW and continue to a ✖ with the `A272`.

The gentle gradient of the East Hampshire downs

3 Cross over and continue ↑ along the SDW, passing through a stand of beech trees, then soon descending steadily to pass some farm buildings and arrive at a ✖. Turn → to continue ↑ on the SDW, taking in a few minor ups and downs, passing through several gates and over several ✖s along the way. After descending a short way across **Gander Down**, pass through a gate and – forking ← – climb a little, passing through another gate. Continue along the field edge and on approaching another gate, swing sharp → along the field edge instead (**this is one of the easiest places to go astray on the whole SDW**). Take the first ← through a gate (*SDW*) and continue to the `A272`.

4 Cross over and continue along a byway track through **Holden Farm**. Continue ↑ along tracks for 1.5km before emerging onto a country road. Continue ↑ for 1km and turn → at a ✖ to pass The Milburys pub, then turn ← at a ✖. Continue along the road (the path runs parallel to the left-hand side of the road, but is **best avoided if there are walkers**) for 1km, then turn → off the road, go through a gate at **Wind Farm**, turn ← and follow signs for the *SDW*. Continue ↑ along a track to **Lomer Farm**; dogleg → then ← then → again to pass through the farmyard and exit along the SDW. Continue along a track before passing through a gate onto a country road. Turn → (↑) along the road and on arriving at a parking area by an area of woodland (the SDW divides into three variants here – one footpath and two bridleways), bear → along the road signposted *Exton*. Turn sharp ← at the first junction and keep ← (↑) at the second.

map continues on p80

map continues on p82

⑤ Descend steadily at first, becoming much steeper, along a narrow road known as The White Way. Shortly after the gradient eases the road bends sharp **right**; continue to a ✖ with Allen's Farm Lane, turn ⬅ then ⬅ again after 200m and continue to a ✖. Turn ➡ onto Beacon Hill Lane and follow this road through the village to the `A32` (at time of writing there were signposts for a *temporary SDW route* through **Exton**). Cross ⬆ over the `A32` and continue along Stock's Lane for 500m, keep ➡ at a fork then turn ⬅ onto a bridleway (SDW) along the wooded dismantled railway line.

⑥ Continue ⬆ for 1km before turning ➡ to drop off the dismantled railway line, staying with the SDW bridleway route. Emerge from woods, turn ➡ along the field edge, then ⬅ before beginning to climb fairly steeply up the western flank of **Old Winchester Hill**. The path levels before climbing more steeply. Turn sharp ➡ to descend a short way along a track then turn sharp ⬅. Continue ⬆ for 700m before turning sharp ⬅ and climbing very steeply for 200m.

⑦ At the top of the climb, the path bears **right** and leads round to a gate near the summit of Old Winchester Hill. Go through and turn ➡ along a bridleway track. Follow the track around to a gate by Old Winchester Hill Lane; don't go through, but turn ⬅ along the bridleway that runs parallel to the road for 500m before crossing over just before a car park, then running along the other side of the road. Go through a gate near the fork in the road.

The variant route on page 84 describes the longer (and tougher) return to Winchester from Leythe House Farm near Petersfield, but for the **shorter return route** take the **LH** fork here along Old Winchester Hill Lane and follow the variant return route description from point 3 (see below).

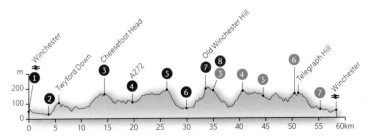

map continues on p84

Descending Limekiln Lane beneath Butser Hill

8 Descend the track across a very steep escarpment – **control your speed** – and pass through a gate at the bottom. Continue ↑ on a track to **Whitewool Farm**, turning ← past a large barn and continuing through the farm, past Meon Springs fishing ponds, before turning → along a farm road at a ✕. After 500m, turn ← along a concrete track and soon begin climbing quite steeply to a ridge. At a ✕ turn → on a tree-lined track along the ridge. Cross ↑ over the road at **Coombe Cross**, to continue on a bridleway and soon begin climbing very steeply along a path up **Salt Hill**, which is very **slippery when wet**.

9 At the top, the path continues along a field edge and passes a radio mast before emerging onto the Droxford Road. Turn ← and continue along the road. At a ✕ bear ← then keep ↑ over two ✕s to continue along a track. Continue ↑ and climb almost imperceptibly for over 2km before arriving at a ✕. Turn ← onto the road and continue towards the summit of **Butser Hill**. Before reaching the car park near the summit, turn ← off the SDW onto a bridleway and descend along Limekiln Lane, steadily at first, becoming steeper. This is an excellent descent, although **tricky in places with ruts and tree roots so control your speed**. Keep ← where the track forks and then levels out before descending steeply again through woods, passing **Leythe House Farm** and emerging onto a road.

To follow the long return variant to Winchester, follow the route description from point **1** below.

10 Turn → along the road then take the first **LH** turn after 400m. Continue to a ✗ and turn ←. Continue ↑ (←) where the road merges, then turn → at the next ✗ to continue through **Ramsdean**. Continue along the road for 2km into **Stroud** and turn → onto the A272 at a ✗ and continue to a major roundabout under the A3 flyover. Negotiate the roundabout anti-clockwise on the pavement and take the fourth exit for **Petersfield**. Continue to a small roundabout and take the second exit, to continue along the A272 to the train station.

Variant return route to Winchester

. . . .

1 From **Leythe House Farm**, turn ← along the road then → onto a bridleway after 500m. Climb a little on the rutted, often muddy, tree-lined Cumber's

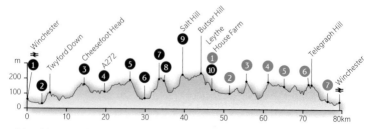

Lane track then descend a little to a ✖. Turn ← along a track and continue ↑ to arrive at a road. Continue ↑ through **Frogmore** then turn → at a junction to continue into **East Meon**. At a ✖ turn → (*West Meon*) and arrive at a ✖ in front of a church. Turn ← and continue out of the village for 1.5km before turning ← onto a byway at **Drayton** (continuing along the road to join the A32 to Warnford is also an option here).

2 Climb steadily, initially on a tarmac road then along a track on Halnaker Lane just inside the edge of **Hen Wood**, ignoring intersecting forestry tracks. Continue to a ✖ at SU 666 217, turn → to rejoin the SDW and descend on a concrete track. At a ✖ turn → on a farm road and continue to a ✖ at **Whitewool Farm**. Turn ← to continue through the farm, then turn → along the SDW on a bridleway track. Turn → through a gate and climb very steeply on a tough, rutted track up along the escarpment. At the top, go through a gate, turn → onto the road and take the **LH** fork.

3 Descend for 2.75km along Old Winchester Hill Lane to arrive at the A32 in **Warnford**. Turn ← along the A32, then take the third **RH** turn by some watercress beds. Continue to **Wheely Down Farm**, then turn ← to follow the MW/SDW variant bridleway through the farm before climbing steeply along a track road. Turn → through a signposted metal gate and keep ← to climb steadily along a grassy hillside. Continue through gates, across fields and into woods through another gate. At the top of the climb, go through a gate and turn → onto a road. Continue for 300m then turn ← (↑) off the road through a gate at a bend (*SDW*).

4 Continue along a track, doglegging ← then → then ← through **Lomer Farm**. Continue, climbing a little to arrive at **Wind Farm**. Turn → and go through a metal gate then turn ← and continue along a road. At a ✖ continue ↑ (leaving the SDW). Continue along the road for 2km, descending a little then climbing to a ✖ at **Lane End Down**. Turn ← (*Owlesbury* and *Upham*) and descend steadily along the road for 600m, turning → onto a bridleway just before the road enters some woods.

5 Descend along a track then level out and continue along the edge of woods before descending again to a ✖. Continue ↑ and climb to a ✖ by a tanker. Bear ← and descend steeply to a ✖. Bear → and climb steeply along a narrow track, which can be **overgrown in summer**. Continue to a ✖ and go ↑ to climb along the edge of woods. The track turns sharp **left** then arrives at a ✖. Turn → and climb steadily towards **Cheesefoot Head**.

6 Just before arriving at the `A272`, turn sharp ← opposite a tanker and drop a short distance along a field edge before turning sharp → and climbing a little to a ✕. Continue ↑ to join the SDW and follow a bridleway around the flank of **Telegraph Hill**, before descending steadily to a ✕ and turning ←. The track then bends **right** to descend to a road. Turn → onto the road and descend steeply through **Chilcomb**. Turn → at the first junction, then → again to continue along King's Lane. The road bends **left** then joins the westbound `A31`; follow the path (*SDW*) along the **LH** side of the road to a roundabout, then follow the path around to the first exit and continue for 200m, doglegging ← then → and → again to cross a bridge over the `M3`.

7 Once across, turn → along a path then bear ← to soon join Petersfield Road. Continue ↑ along the road to a ✕ with East Hill. Bear ← and descend to the next ✕ and turn second → to follow Chesil Street into the town centre. Turn ← off a roundabout onto High Street, then continue ↑ over the next roundabout along The Broadway. Where The Broadway becomes the (pedestrianised) High Street again, turn → onto Middle Brook Street, then ← to continue ↑ along St George's Street as far as the ✕ with Jewry Street. Fork ← then bear → to rejoin the High Street. Continue ↑ to a roundabout at West Gate, then turn → and continue ↑ before forking → onto Station Road to arrive at the train station.

The fast descent through Charlton Forest (Route 8)

Routes around **Chichester & Petersfield**

Climbing towards the South Downs Way in Singleton Forest

Route 7

Westdean Woods and Cocking Down

7

START/FINISH	Cocking Hilltop car park SU 875 167. The nearest train station is Chichester (see page 39).
DISTANCE	21.5km (13½ miles)
ON ROAD	3km (2 miles)
OFF ROAD	18.5km (11½ miles)
VARIANT	26.5km (16½ miles) with additional loop around Levin Down
ON ROAD	4.5km (2¾ miles)
OFF ROAD	22km (13¾ miles)
ASCENT	515m (1690ft); Levin Down loop 610m (2005ft)
GRADE	▲
TIME	2–2hrs 30mins (add 30mins for Levin Down loop)
PUB	The Bluebell at Cocking, The Royal Oak at Hooksway
CAFÉ	Moonlight Café at Cocking, Studio Tearooms at Singleton

85%
OFF ROAD

Overview

This circular route climbs along Cocking Down heading west along a fine section of the South Downs Way (SDW) to Treyford Hill before descending precipitously to Hooksway, then heading southeast via Philliswood Lane and Chilgrove. From Chilgrove, country lanes lead northeast to Westdean woods, where forestry tracks take you uphill then down to cross the A286. It's then up and down then up again through Nightingale Woods and Singleton Forest before rejoining the SDW to make a final long descent back to Hilltop car park. An additional variant route takes in a loop around Levin Down. There are several noteworthy climbs: a long steep climb up Cocking Down; a long, gradual climb through Westdean Woods on forest tracks; a short, steep climb up through Nightingale Woods; and a long steep climb on a rough forest track from Burntoak Gate to the SDW. The route mostly follows well-maintained bridleways and byways, although there are short road sections near Chilgrove and Wolverstone Farm. Some sections of this route, particularly on the SDW, are popular with walkers, horse riders and other users. There are some fast descents on this route, so for your own safety – and that of other users – control your speed.

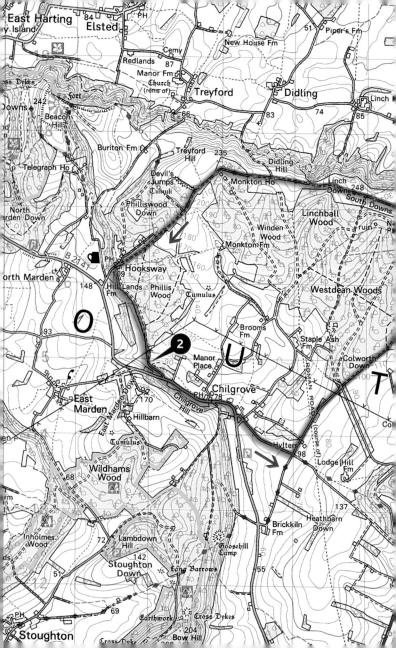

Directions

1 From the car park, turn ← onto the SDW, continue **W** past some livestock sheds and climb, initially on a farm road. As the gradient steepens and farm road gives way to chalk track, keep → (↑) at a fork and continue to climb over **Cocking Down**.

Continue ↑ on the SDW as the gradient eases. Cross Linch Ball then **Didling Hill**, enter woods and swing **SW** along the flank of **Treyford Hill**. Descend through woods, continue ↑ at a ✗ (leaving the SDW) and continue steeply downhill along the byway to **Hooksway**. As the descent bottoms out, turn ← opposite the Royal Oak pub onto a bridleway and continue along Philliswood Lane. After 1.2km, the track climbs gradually to the B2141.

2 Turn ← along the road for 1.2km, then take the second ← onto a minor road at **Chilgrove**. Continue ↑ over a ✗ then turn ← at the next ✗ onto Hylter's Lane. Continue past Hylter's Farm and at a ✗ continue ↑ on a bridleway, climbing across **Colworth Down** and into **Westdean Woods**, initially on a forestry track. Continue ↑ to a ✗ at SU 860 158.

3 Turn → onto a forestry track then bear → off the track onto a bridleway entering the woods. Descend through woods, gradually at first but becoming steeper. Eventually, the bridleway briefly intersects with a forestry track, before you turn → again to descend steeply through woods to the A286 – **slow down** as the bridleway emerges directly onto a road with fast-moving traffic. Turn → along the road for 300m then turn ← off it and join a bridleway to the **left** that climbs steeply through woods. Dogleg ← then → over a forestry track and continue to climb through Nightingale Wood. The track levels and descends, initially through woods then on a flinty track, to **Broadham House**. Climb ↑ up a grass slope to go through a gate and arrive at a ✗.

Climbing a forest track near Hooksway

Quiet country road near Charlton

Variant: additional loop around Levin Down

1 This loop extends the route by 5km and 30mins. Turn → through a metal gate and climb steadily along the obvious path across the grassy flank of **Levin Down**. The path levels, continues through a gate then descends fairly steeply to go through two gates close together. Continue descending along a track lane to emerge at the A286 – **beware fast-moving traffic** – turn ← and descend along the road to **Singleton**. Turn ← at a ✗ in the village, keep ← at the next ✗ and continue along Charlton Road. Just before **Charlton**, turn ← onto North Lane (*Downs Bridleway*) and continue along a flinty track. After 1.2km, turn ← off North Lane on a bridleway, which turns sharp **right** and climbs steeply to a ✗ at which the variant rejoins the main route.

4 Turn ← (↑ if following variant) to head **N** along a bridleway to a ✗ at **Burntoak Gate** then begin to climb steeply ↑ on a rough track through **Singleton Forest**. After climbing for 1km, the bridleway bends **NE** at a ✗ and continues climbing steeply, before emerging from the woods at a ✗ with the SDW along the ridge. Turn ← along the SDW and soon begin the long descent, steadily at first but becoming much steeper, before passing through a gate, continuing through a farm and then along Hillbarn Lane as the track levels. Cross ↑ over the A286 to return to Hilltop car park.

Woodland singletrack near Heyshott Down

8

Route 8

Heyshott Down and Charlton Forest

START/FINISH	Cocking Hilltop car park SU 875 167. The nearest train station is Chichester (see page 39).
DISTANCE	18km (11 miles)
ON ROAD	2km (1¼ miles)
OFF ROAD	16km (9¾ miles)
ASCENT	555m (1815ft)
GRADE	▲
TIME	2hrs–2hrs 30mins
PUB	The Bluebell at Cocking, The Fox Goes Free at Charlton
CAFÉ	Moonlight Café at Cocking, Studio Tearooms at Singleton

Overview

This route takes in some tough climbs, several excellent descents, plenty of forest trails and a downland village or two. A long, steep climb up Manorfarm Down on the South Downs Way (SDW) is soon followed by a very steep descent of Heyshott Down then one of the toughest climbs on the whole South Downs. Several slightly less challenging uphills include a steady climb over

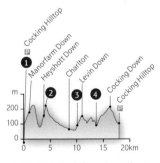

the grassy slopes of Levin Down from the A286; a gradual climb from Broadham House into Nightingale Wood and a long, steady climb along forest tracks from Wolverstone Farm on the A286 to the SDW atop Cocking Down. The route mostly follows well-maintained bridleways and byways, although there are short road sections near Singleton and Wolverstone Farm. Some sections of this route, including the SDW, are popular with walkers, horse riders and other users. There are some fast descents on this route, so for your own safety and that of other users – control your speed.

Directions

1 From Hilltop car park, cross ↑ over the `A286` to join the SDW along Hillbarn Lane. Continue through the farm at **Hill Barn** and begin to climb steeply on chalk track, passing through a metal gate. Climb steeply up **Manorfarm Down** for a further 1 km until the path levels. Continue along the SDW to a ✖ at a bend in the track. Turn ← through a gate and descend diagonally across a field. Go through another gate – a waymarker indicates the *New Lipchis Way* (NLW) – and descend very steeply through woods along

Heyshott Down – **make sure your brakes are sharp** before attempting this descent. The gradient eases as the track leaves the woods and bears **left**. Continue descending along a rutted track, turning → at a ✕ and then → again at the next ✕ shortly after. Begin the long climb back to the SDW, steadily at first, becoming very steep and continuing for what seems a long way, before passing through a gate, levelling out and crossing a field to another gate.

2 Go through and cross straight over the SDW into woods to join a singletrack bridleway and begin the long descent through **Charlton Forest**. After 1.5km, the bridleway swings **right** to join a wider track, before emerging from woods and continuing to descend more gradually, winding along a valley on the North Lane track, eventually arriving at a ✕ at the **W** end of **Charlton** village. Turn → and continue along the road to **Singleton**; bear → at a fork to arrive at a ✕ with the `A286`. Turn → along the road – **beware fast-moving traffic** – for 300m, climbing to a hill brow then turning → onto a bridleway.

3 Climb fairly steeply along the track, passing through two gates close together, and continue up along a grassy slope along the flank of **Levin Down** on the NLW. The path climbs, passes through a gate, levels out and then descends steadily to a ✕ next to a disused quarry. Go through a gate, turn ← through the next gate and descend a slope to **Broadham House**. Continue ↑ on a bridleway, climbing steadily along a flinty track. Where the track bends, take the **RH** fork to stay on the bridleway (**probably no signpost**) through the woods – this is **easy to miss** because going straight ahead on the left-hand fork seems the obvious choice. Continue climbing a little further through woods before descending quite steeply to arrive at a forest track. Dogleg ← then → to rejoin the bridleway and descend steeply through woods to arrive at the `A286`.

4 Turn → along the road – **beware fast-moving traffic** – and continue for 300m before turning ← off the road onto a bridleway just before and opposite **Wolverstone Farm**. Climb steeply through woods to join a forestry track briefly before bearing ← through woods, again on a bridleway. Continue ↑ and climb steadily for over 1km before the gradient eases. The path briefly rejoins the forestry track before arriving at a ✕. Turn → then ← at a fork and continue climbing steadily through woods to a ✕. Turn → and descend, initially through woods, before emerging onto **Cocking Down** and continuing to descend to a ✕. Turn → to continue descending steeply on the SDW, passing some livestock sheds, then turning → into Hilltop car park.

Climbing the wooded lane near Chalton

9

Route 9

Petersfield – Beacon Hill Circuit

Start/Finish	Petersfield train station SU 744 236
Distance	38.5km (24 miles)
On road	17km (10½ miles)
Off road	21.5km (13½ miles)
Ascent	895m (2940ft)
Grade	▲
Time	3hrs–4hrs
Pub	Various in Petersfield, The Red Lion at Chalton, The Victoria Inn at West Marden, The Five Bells and The Master Robert at Buriton
Café	Various in Petersfield; QECP Visitor Centre, Buriton

Overview

This route takes in a sizeable loop around the Downs south of Petersfield. As well as tackling a very challenging route up to the whale-backed summit

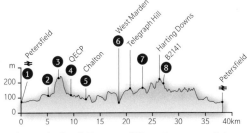

of Butser Hill – the highest point on the South Downs at 270m – the route calls in briefly at Queen Elizabeth Country Park (QECP) before stringing together a fine collection of bridleways, lanes and byways through the villages of Chalton and West Marden and onwards to join the South Downs Way (SDW) near Beacon Hill. The route continues west along the SDW, crossing Harting Downs and following byways and country lanes back to the edge of QECP before descending through Buriton to return to Petersfield. There are several noteworthy climbs: the ascent of Butser Hill on an almost impossibly steep chalk track (an alternative is supplied); a fairly steep climb up a wooded escarpment on the way to West Marden; a steep climb up little Round Down; and a steep climb up Harting Downs. Although almost half the route is on roads, most of these are quiet country lanes.

Directions

1 From the station entrance, turn ← then ← again onto the `A272`. At a small roundabout, turn ← (*Stroud*). Continue to a major roundabout, pass under a flyover and take the `A272` exit. Continue into the village of **Stroud** and turn ← (*Ramsdean*). Continue along the road for 2km, passing through **Ramsdean**, before arriving at a ✕. Turn ← and continue, ignoring a right-hand fork, to another ✕. Here there are two options. The main route presents you with one of the most challenging climbs on the South Downs so there is no shame in choosing the alternative.

2 If opting to tackle the mother of all climbs, continue ↑ over the ✕ onto a byway along a track. This is straightforward at first, but as you continue along to Rake Bottom you will see the chalk track ahead climbing steeply up the flank of **Butser Hill** (270m). This steep, narrow track would be enough of a challenge without the **rut running along its middle**. If you do manage to reach the top still in the saddle, there is a nasty collection of **tree roots to negotiate** before the track intersects with Limekiln Lane and continues to climb on a fairly steep gradient to join the SDW at a ✕ with a minor road.

Variant route via Limekiln Lane

1 If the route up Butser Hill from Rake Bottom is too daunting, turn → at the ✕ (*Oxenbourne*), continue for 600m then turn ← onto the Limekiln Lane byway at **Leythe House Farm**.
Continue past farm buildings, then climb very steeply into woods as the track bends **right** then **left**, leaving the woods as the gradient eases. Continue climbing on a **rutted and tree-root criss-crossed** track, which levels for a while then climbs steadily again before arriving at a ✕ with a minor road and joining the SDW.

Climbing towards Butser Hill, the highest hill on the South Downs at 270m

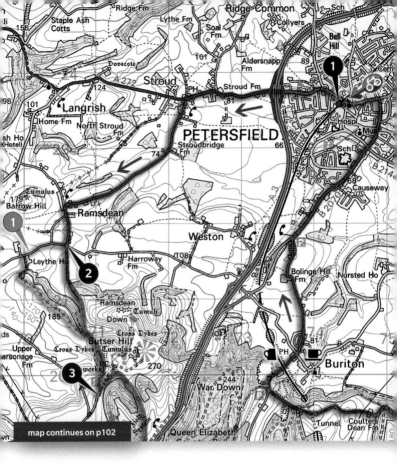

3 Turn ← onto the road for a short distance, bear → onto a bridleway (SDW) and continue to a gate. Go through and follow the obvious track as it descends, gradually at first, becoming much steeper, along the grassy **S** flank of Butser Hill. Go through a gate halfway down and continue to descend the grassy slope to a gate at the field edge. Go through and continue up a slight rise, cross ↑ over two tracks – following signs for the *SDW* – and join the slip road to descend under the A3 road bridge.

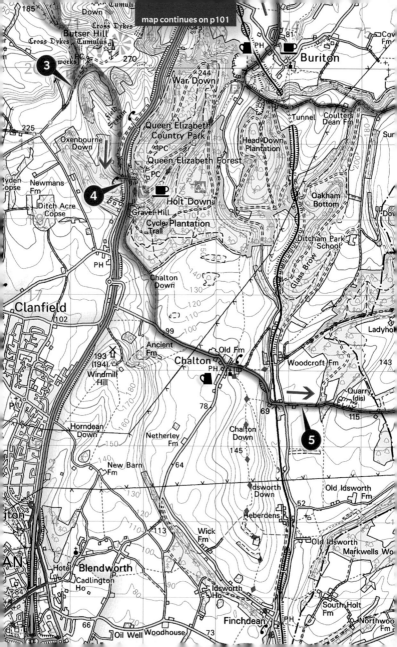

map continues on p101

3

Butser Hill

Cross Dykes

Cross Dykes

Tumulus

185

Down

Cumulus

Tumulus

works

270

225

Oxenbourne
Down

Newmans
Fm

Ditch Acre
Copse

PH

War Down

244

Queen Elizabeth
Country Park

PC

Queen Elizabeth Forest

PC

4

Holt Down

Gravel Hill

Cycle Plantation
Trail

Chalton
Down

140

130

120

110

100

Clanfield

102

99

Ancient
Fm

193
(194)

Windmill
Hill

180

170

160

150

140

New Barn
Fm

64

Horndean
Down

Netherley
Fm

130

120

110

113

Wick
Fm

Chalton

PH

78

Old Fm

Chalton
Down

145

dsworth
Down

Buriton

81

PH

Tunnel

Coulters
Dean Fm

Head Down
Plantation

Oakham
Bottom

Ditcham Park
School

Glass Brow

Ladyho

Woodcroft Fm

143

Quarry
(dis)

69

115

5

52

Old Idsworth
Fm

Heberdens

Old Idsworth

Markwells Wo

Hotel

Blendworth

Cadlington
Ho

66

Oil Well Woodhouse

90

Idsworth
Ho

Finchdean

73

PH

South Holt
Fm

Northwoo
Fm

Cov
Fm

Sur

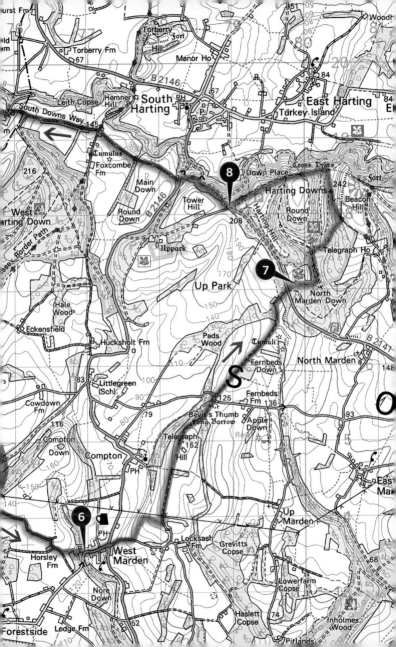

Bridleway signpost near North Marden Down

4 Continue ↑ into the QECP car park and pass around to the → of the visitor centre and café, to continue ↑ along the road past parking and picnicking areas. Where the road bends **left**, turn → then ← (leaving the SDW) to continue past maintenance buildings on a bridleway. Continue ↑ along the bridleway track running along the edge of QECP, before crossing **Chalton Down** to arrive at Chalton Lane. Turn ← along the road and continue to **Chalton** village. At a ✗ before the pub, turn ← (*Ditcham* and *Idsworth*) and climb a little before descending steeply. At the bottom of the descent, the road turns sharp **left** and continues to a ✗.

5 Continue ↑ over the ✗ onto Huckswood Lane track, which soon climbs a little. After 1.7km, turn → at the first bridleway ✗ and descend through arable fields on a bumpy track. Go up a slight rise through a copse to a road, dogleg → then ← through a gate onto a bridleway and cross a field on a rise. Enter woods, bear → and climb fairly steeply. Continue ↑ past an intersecting bridleway on the left as the track levels, then follow the bridleway as it leads around to the **left** on an old drovers' road. Follow the winding bridleway, bearing → at a ✗ with a footpath after 1.2km and ← at a second shortly after. Continue ↑ and **watch out for a bridleway sign on**

the left at the edge of the woods. Take this turning to descend a track steeply through woods, emerging onto a road just before **West Marden**.

6 Turn ← to continue through the village to a ✖ and go ↑ to climb steeply along a country road. Take the first bridleway track signposted on the ← and continue to climb fairly steeply. After 400m, the bridleway turns sharp **right** – continue ↑ then take the second ←. Continue along flinty track, crossing over **Telegraph Hill** before descending fairly steeply, then crossing ↑ over a minor road by **Bevis's Thumb**. Continue ↑ along a bridleway for 1.5km, swinging → as the path gives way to a broad chalk track before arriving at the B2141 . Dogleg ← then → to pick up a bridleway on the other side of the road by Kill Devil Copse.

7 Jink → onto the bridleway and continue ↑. Drop down a slope, turn ← through a gate and descend steeply through woods to the valley floor. Continue ↑ to a ✖ and turn → to climb steeply up Little Round Down. Turn ← onto the SDW at the top of the climb and immediately descend again to the saddle between **Beacon Hill** and Harting Downs. Turn ← and climb to a gate, go through and climb very steeply up to the top of **Harting Downs**. Once up, continue along the ridge before descending a little past a car park to arrive at the B2141 .

8 Cross the road to rejoin the bridleway and descend through woods to the B2146 . Cross over and continue along the SDW byway on Forty Acre Lane (from here to QECP, the SDW follows broad farm tracks and stretches of minor road, so **beware farm and other traffic**). Continue ↑ over a ✖ and along a track, climbing a little at Hundred Acres before descending steeply to a road. Bear ← along the road, past **Sunwood Farm**, climb a little and bear → at a fork. Descend through woods and continue along a winding narrow road to a ✖ opposite the QECP car park at Kiln Lane. Turn → and descend steeply on the road, under a railway bridge and through Buriton village. Continue ↑ on a narrow winding country road to arrive at the B2070 . Turn → along the road to return to Petersfield, keeping → at roundabouts. Continue ↑ into town and follow signs for the railway station.

Climbing along forest track in Kingley Vale

Route 10

Chichester – Charlton Forest Circuit

START/FINISH	Chichester train station SU 858 044
DISTANCE	42km (26 miles)
ON ROAD	3km (2 miles)
OFF ROAD	39km (24 miles)
ASCENT	800m (2625ft)
GRADE	▲
TIME	3hrs–4hrs
PUB	Various in Chichester, The Fox Goes Free at Charlton
CAFÉ	Various in Chichester, Moonlight Café at Cocking

Overview

This circular route heads out to (and returns from) the Downs along the Centurion Way (Regional Cycle Route 88), which follows the course of

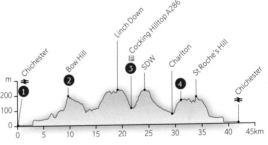

the disused Chichester to Midhurst railway line. The route then heads for the wooded hills of Kingley Vale northwest of Chichester, before descending to Hooksway and climbing to join the South Downs Way (SDW). A sublime section along the Downland ridge follows before a fast descent to Cocking then a stiff climb up Manorfarm Down. The SDW is abandoned on a long descent through Charlton Forest to Charlton Village, from where the Chalk Road bridleway winds up to Goodwood Race Course. There is a final climb up and around St Roche's Hill before a fine descent to the Lavant Valley and the return to Chichester along the Centurion Way (CW). The route mostly follows well-maintained bridleways and byways, although there are short road sections near Chilgrove and Goodwood. Some sections of this route, particularly Kingley Vale and the SDW, are popular with walkers, horse riders and other users.

Directions

1 Exit the station and follow signs for National Cycle Route 2, also known as the South Coast Cycle Route. At Westgate, by the entrance to Bishop Luffa School, turn ➔ onto the CW, which follows the course of a disused railway. Continue along the CW for around 6km, turning ← onto a bridleway near Binderton. Continue to the `A286`, turn ➔ onto the road then dogleg ← onto a lane and pass **Binderton House**. Follow the road as it climbs, bends (ignore the bridleway straight ahead) and descends to the `B2141` at Welldown. Turn ➔ onto the road then dogleg ← to join a bridleway. Climb steadily along the track to a ✗ on the saddle between Stoke Clump and Bow Hill. Turn ➔ and climb, steadily at first then ever more steeply, as you enter woods at Kingley Vale nature reserve, continuing to a ✗ just below and **NE** of the summit of **Bow Hill**.

2 Turn ➔ at a ✗ and continue along the ridge for 2.5km, descending very gradually, keeping ↑ over ✗s until arriving at

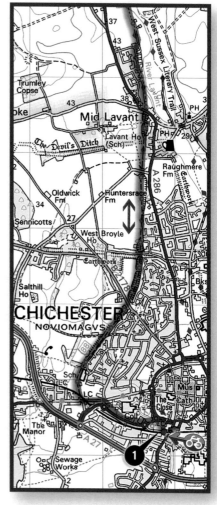

map continues on p110

map continues on p108

a ✖ at SU 828 139. Turn → onto a loose asphalt track and descend the steep NE escarpment of **Chilgrove Hill**. At the bottom, turn ← onto the `B2141` and continue for 700m along the road before turning → onto a bridleway. Descend gradually along Philliswood Lane before entering woods near **Hooksway**. Emerge onto a minor road opposite the Royal Oak pub, turn → and at a ✖ take the **RH** byway (indicated with a *purple arrow* on a signpost) and climb steadily to a ✖ with the SDW. Keep ↑ and continue climbing gently around the flank of Treyford Hill. As the SDW bends E, continue along the ridge, over **Didling Hill** and Linch Ball before descending steeply over **Cocking Down** on a chalk track that gives way to a farm road. Pass livestock sheds before arriving at the `A286`.

3 Cross the road – **beware fast-moving traffic** – and continue ↑ along Hillbarn Lane on the SDW before beginning the long, steep climb up **Manorfarm Down**. When the gradient eventually eases, continue ↑ to the second bridleway ✖ at SU 904 165. Turn → into the woods on a singletrack bridleway and begin the long descent through **Charlton Forest**. After 1.5km, the bridleway swings **right** to join a wider track, before emerging from the woods and continuing to descend more gradually, winding along a valley on the North Lane track and eventually arriving at the village of **Charlton**. Turn ← on Charlton Road into the village, then first → and second ← along a lane to join the Chalk Road bridleway, which heads **S** out of the village before winding steeply up to the ridge between **Charlton Park** and **Goodwood Country Park**.

4 Where the bridleway reaches the road running along the ridge turn → to follow the road past Goodwood Race Course. At a T-junction, turn → up the hill then, after 300m, ← into a parking area. Join the bridleway through the woods that leads to the **left** of the parking area, climbing steeply at first, passing through a gate, then swinging around the **S** flank of **St Roche's Hill**. Pass through a car park and continue ↑ over a ✖ onto a bridleway. Take the **LH** fork to join the West Sussex Literary Trail (WSLT). Descend steeply along the field edge, through a gate and down a grassy hillside to a ✖ then continue ↑ through a gate, leaving the WSLT. Cross a bridge over a disused railway and turn sharp ← to a ✖ (rejoining the CW) and retrace your outward route to Chichester station.

Bridleway in Kingley Vale Nature Reserve

Route 11

Petersfield – Singleton Forest Circuit

START/FINISH	Petersfield train station SU 744 236 or Harting Downs car park SU 791 180
DISTANCE	54.5km (34 miles)
ON ROAD	20.5km (12¾ miles)
OFF ROAD	34km (21¼ miles)
ASCENT	1310m (4290ft)
GRADE	◆
TIME	4–5hrs
PUB	Various in Petersfield and South Harting, The Bluebell at Cocking, The Fox Goes Free at Charlton
CAFÉ	Various in Petersfield, Moonlight Café at Cocking

60% OFF ROAD

Overview

This long and tough circular route takes in a large loop of the Downs southeast of Petersfield. Starting from Petersfield and gaining the ridge west of Harting Downs, the route heads east along one of the finest stretches of the South Downs Way (SDW), taking in a collection of hilltops before descending at Cocking Down, crossing the A286 and climbing along Manorfarm Down to Heyshott Down. The route then plummets through Singleton Forest to Charlton before climbing to Goodwood Race Course, continuing over St Roche's Hill, crossing the Lavant

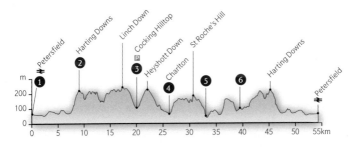

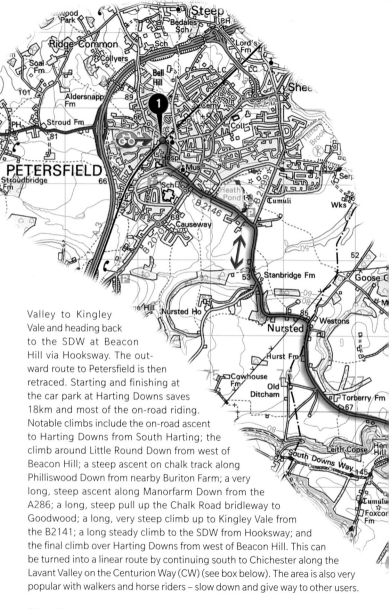

Valley to Kingley
Vale and heading back
to the SDW at Beacon
Hill via Hooksway. The outward route to Petersfield is then
retraced. Starting and finishing at
the car park at Harting Downs saves
18km and most of the on-road riding.
Notable climbs include the on-road ascent
to Harting Downs from South Harting; the
climb around Little Round Down from west of
Beacon Hill; a steep ascent on chalk track along
Philliswood Down from nearby Buriton Farm; a very
long, steep ascent along Manorfarm Down from the
A286; a long, steep pull up the Chalk Road bridleway to
Goodwood; a long, very steep climb up to Kingley Vale from
the B2141; a long steady climb to the SDW from Hooksway; and
the final climb over Harting Downs from west of Beacon Hill. This can
be turned into a linear route by continuing south to Chichester along the
Lavant Valley on the Centurion Way (CW) (see box below). The area is also very
popular with walkers and horse riders – slow down and give way to other users.

map continues on p115

Directions

1 From the station entrance, continue ↑ past Cycleworks bike shop along Lavant Road. Turn first → along Charles Street then bear ← along the `B2146` Sussex Road and continue ↑ on this road as it leaves town. Keep ↑ on the `B2146` through **Nursted** and on to **South Harting**. Arriving at a ✕ in South Harting, turn → to continue **S** out of the village on the `B2146`. Climb steeply up the **N** escarpment of the Downs, bearing ← onto the `B2141` at a fork. Continue climbing very steeply until the gradient eases, then turn ← off the road onto the SDW beside the alternative start/finish point at Harting Downs car park. Climb steadily to **Harting Downs**.

2 Continue along the ridge before descending steeply along a chalk track to a gate. Go through and descend a little further to a ✕. Turn → along the SDW and climb steeply around the **W** flank of **Beacon Hill**. At a ✕ turn ← along the **E** flank of Beacon Hill, then descend to a ✕ and continue ↑ to climb steeply up and over Pen Hill. Descend to the edge of the woods, turn → then keep ↑ over a ✕ to continue on the SDW. At the next ✕ (near **Buriton Farm**) dogleg ← then → and soon begin climbing, steadily at first, becoming steeper on chalk track. Keep ← at a fork shortly before the gradient eases then levels. At the next ✕ turn ← and climb gently around the flank of **Treyford Hill**. As the SDW bends **E**, continue along the ridge, over **Didling Hill** and Linch Ball before descending steeply over **Cocking Down** on a chalk track that gives way to a farm road. Pass livestock sheds before arriving at the `A286`.

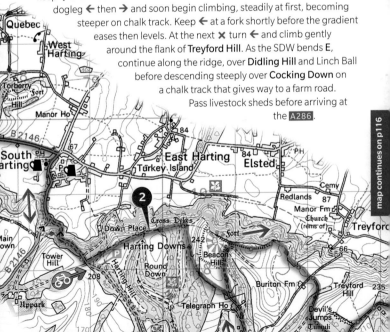

map continues on p116

The view east across the Downs from Pen Hill

3 Cross the road – **beware fast-moving traffic** – and continue ↑ along Hillbarn
Lane before beginning the long, steep climb up **Manorfarm Down**. When
the gradient eventually eases, continue ↑ on the SDW to the first bridleway
✗. Turn → and descend into woods on a track that becomes **steep and very
rutted in places**. Continue ↑ at a ✗ then bear slightly ← at a fork to stay
on the bridleway and continue descending through **Singleton Forest**. The
track eventually levels out and emerges from the woods at **Burntoak Gate**.
Continue ↑ to a ✗ at the foot of **Levin Down** and bear ← to descend steeply
on a flint track. The track levels and turns sharp **left** to a ✗. Turn → to
continue along the valley floor on the winding North Lane track, eventually
arriving at the village of **Charlton**.

4 Go ← on Charlton Road through the village, then first → and second ←
along a lane to join the Chalk Road bridleway, which heads S out of the
village before winding steeply up to the ridge between **Charlton Park** and
Goodwood Country Park. Where the bridleway reaches the road running
along the ridge, turn → to follow the road past Goodwood Racecourse. At a
T-junction, turn → up the hill then, after 300m, ← into a parking area. Join a

Bridleway through woodland in Kingley Vale

bridleway through the woods that leads to the **left** of the parking area, climbing steeply at first, passing through a gate, then swinging around the S flank of **St Roche's Hill**. Pass through a car park and continue ↑ over a ✖ onto a bridleway. Take the **LH** fork to join the West Sussex Literary Trail (WSLT). Descend steeply along a field edge, through a gate and down a grassy hillside to a ✖ and continue ↑ through a gate, leaving the WSLT.

To turn this into a linear route to Chichester, cross a bridge over the disused railway, turn sharp ← and continue **S** along the Centurion Way for 6km. Turn → by the entrance to Bishop Luffa School at Westgate and follow National Cycle Route 2 signs to the train station (saves 15km, or a total route length of 39.5km). There are services to London, Brighton and Southampton; change at Eastleigh for Petersfield.

5 Cross the bridge over a disused railway and continue ↑ through a gate to the A286 . Turn → onto the road and then ← onto a lane and pass **Binderton House**. Where the road bends **left**, continue ↑ on Binderton Lane bridleway; pass a house, cross ↑ over a farm track and descend quite steeply along a bumpy bridleway to the B2141 . Turn → on the road then, after 150m, ← onto a bridleway. Go through a metal stock gate, then follow a fence along the edge of the field (**muddy in winter**) to pick up a track. Climb steadily at first, soon becoming very steep as the track enters woods. Turn →

at the second ✖ and continue along the ridge, descending very gradually until arriving at a ✖ at SU 828 139. Turn → onto a loose asphalt track and descend the steep **NE** escarpment of **Chilgrove Hill**. At the bottom, turn ← onto the `B2141` and continue for 700m before turning → onto a bridleway.

6 Descend gradually along Philliswood Lane before entering woods at **Hooksway**. Emerge onto a minor road opposite the Royal Oak pub, turn ← along the road and climb steeply, turning → onto a bridleway before the brow of the hill. Continue ↑ on a gentle gradient, briefly turning sharp ← then → again. Continue ← at a fork and soon pass through a gate to emerge onto an asphalt estate road. Continue ↑ and fork → to go through a gate at the top of the road. Turn ← at a bridleway fork to rejoin the SDW. Continue along Little Round Down before descending steeply to the saddle **W** of **Beacon Hill**. At the ✖ on the saddle, turn ← on the SDW and climb steeply, passing through a gate, up to **Harting Downs**. Continue along the ridge before descending steadily, passing a car park, to the `B2141`. Turn → to descend steeply to South Harting and retrace your outward route along the `B2146` to Petersfield.

Approaching Wepham Down along rollercoaster chalk track (Route 16)

Climbing Bignor Hill gives a great view east along the main ridge of the South Downs

12

Route 12

Amberley and Houghton Forest

START/FINISH	Amberley train station TQ 026 118
DISTANCE	15km (9½ miles)
ON ROAD	2km (1¼ miles)
OFF ROAD	13km (8¼ miles)
ASCENT	380m (1255ft)
GRADE	■
TIME	1hr–1hr 30mins
PUB	The Bridge Inn at Amberley, The George and Dragon at Houghton
CAFÉ	Riverside Café at Amberley

85% OFF ROAD

Overview

This is a shorter route centred around Houghton Forest to the northwest of Arundel. Much of the route follows bridleways and forest tracks – it's worth carrying a compass or GPS. In winter, some sections of the route, particularly those in woodland, are prone to churning up. There are two big

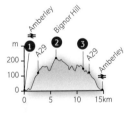

climbs: a winding ascent – steep in places – on chalk track from Houghton Lane to the A29 near the beginning and a steep pull up Bignor Hill from the foot of Westburton Hill. Watch out and slow down for horse riders and walkers.

Directions

1 Exit the train station, turning ← onto the B2139, and head for **Houghton**, 800m along the road. Turn → onto Houghton Lane and descend along a minor road to a ✕ with the South Downs Way (SDW). Turn ← and climb steadily at first on a winding chalk track that steepens considerably, then eases again before reaching the A29. Cross over, turn → and continue a short way along a track by the roadside before turning ← onto the bridleway (SDW). Climb gradually on chalk track, then contour along before

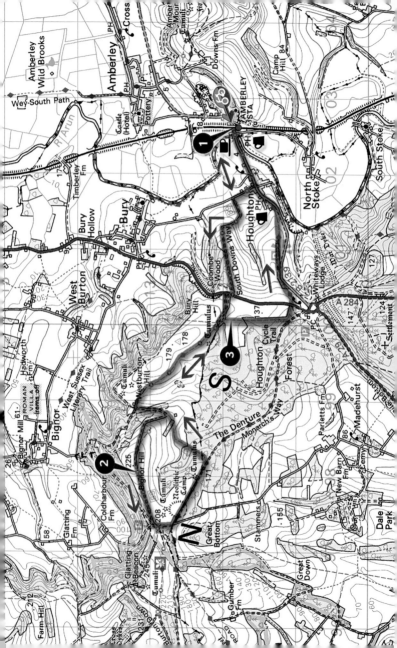

descending and passing some livestock sheds to arrive at a ✖. Turn ← and climb steeply on chalk track. At the next ✖ turn → and continue climbing steeply to cross the summit of **Bignor Hill** (225m).

Descending from Westburton Hill

2 Descend steadily to a ✖ with a minor road next to a parking area. Pass the parking area and turn first ← onto a bridleway. Continue to a ✖ and turn ← onto the Monarch's Way (MW). Descend steadily on a bridleway for 1km, passing through woodlands along **The Denture**, then turn ← into woods on another bridleway. The forest track soon begins to descend steeply and where it bottoms out and swings **left**, keep ↑ on a bridleway exiting the woods and dropping into an arable field before climbing fairly steeply out the other side. Join a farm track where the climb eases and continue to a ✖. Take the **RH** fork to descend steeply on a chalk track. At a ✖ at the bottom of the descent, turn → to pass some livestock sheds and continue ↑ on the SDW, retracing your inward route as far as the next ✖.

3 Turn ← onto a bridleway, leaving the SDW, and descend along the edge of **Houghton Forest**. After almost 1km the track bends sharp **left**, rejoins the MW and continues to the A29 – keep ↑ and don't bend right before reaching the road. Cross the road – **beware fast-moving traffic** – and descend on a bridleway through woods, then along a field edge before crossing a private driveway and descending through woods to join the road near the George and Dragon pub. Turn ← along the road to return for 1km to Amberley train station.

Heading along The Denture

Climbing up to the SDW from Buddington Bottom

Route 13

Worthing – Chanctonbury Ring Circuit

START/FINISH	Worthing train station TQ 146 034
DISTANCE	25km (15½ miles)
ON ROAD	5km (3 miles)
OFF ROAD	20km (12½ miles)
ASCENT	545m (1790ft)
GRADE	■
TIME	2hrs–2hrs 30mins
PUB	Various in Worthing
CAFÉ	Various in Worthing

80% OFF ROAD

Overview

This circular route loops around the Downs above Worthing, taking in the Iron Age hill forts of Cissbury Ring and Chanctonbury Ring, as well as fine Downland ridges, coombes and woodland. The route goes through some beautiful countryside and there are fine views across the Downs, the Low Weald and the Channel coast. Most of the route follows

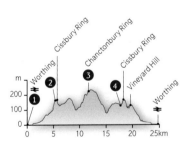

well-maintained bridleways including a brief spell on the South Downs Way (SDW). There are three major climbs: a steady 2km climb to Cissbury Ring from the A27, a steep climb up to the SDW from Buddington Bottom and another up the flank of Vineyard Hill to the south of Cissbury Ring. Conditions are generally good, although some bridleways can become muddy and churned up after wet weather. Watch out for horse riders and walkers especially along the SDW.

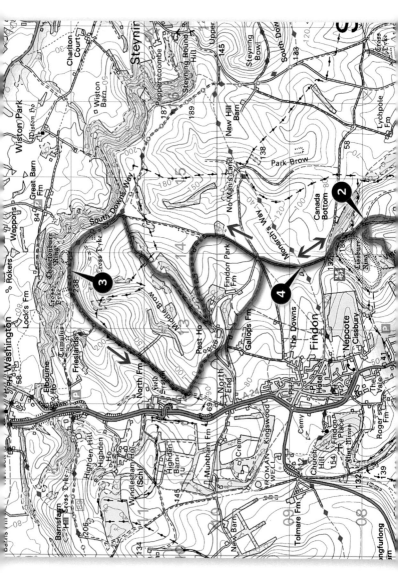

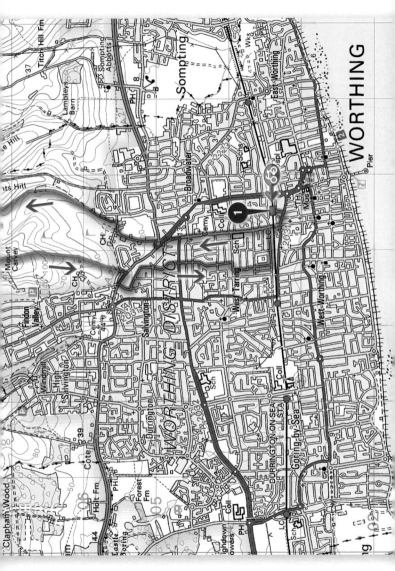

Passing the wooded Iron Age hill fort of Chanctonbury Ring

Directions

1 From the station entrance, follow the one-way street **S** for 150m to a **✗** with the `A2031`. Turn **→** then **→** again at a mini-roundabout, then continue **↑** and **N** for 1.5km to a **✗** with the `A24`. Turn **←** and continue **NW** along the `A24` to a major roundabout junction of the `A24`/`A27`. Take the second exit **←** onto a residential road at TQ 141 050. Continue **N** past houses and playing fields. The road bends **right** after 500m, and after another 150m turn **←** onto a track, which soon becomes a bridleway. Climb gradually at first on a chalk track, then steeply above Deep Bottom to arrive at the **E** edge of **Cissbury Ring**.

2 Go through a gate and continue **↑** on the main track around the **NE** ramparts of the Iron Age hill fort to a gate at a **✗**. Go through and descend steeply to a gate. Go through, continue **↑** over a **✗** and through a parking area. Continue **↑** over a **✗** (after 400m) then **↑** over a second **✗** after a further 500m, following the **RH** fork just beyond the initial **✗**. Continue **↑** then, shortly after the track enters some woods, take the **LH** fork and soon descend steeply to arrive at a metal gate. Don't go through, but turn sharp **→** and continue along Buddington Bottom, eventually climbing, initially on a wooded lane, to arrive at a ✖ with the SDW. Turn ← to climb on a broad flinty track, cross a cattle grid and follow the track as it curves past the wooded Iron Age hill fort of **Chanctonbury Ring**.

❸ Continue along the flint and chalk bridleway, crossing another cattle grid then descending a little as the path begins to bend **SW**. Continue ↑ (**leaving the SDW**, which bends sharp right) and begin to descend more steeply. The path forks briefly then rejoins again. Descend for 1.5km on an excellent track, turning ← at the first ✖. The path drops again then climbs a little towards **Pest House**. Turn → onto a concrete track before reaching farm buildings and climb to a ✖. Go through a gate ↑ and climb the obvious path across a field, then go through another gate and turn ← at a ✖. Continue past a house and paddocks onto a singletrack bridleway, keep ↑ before merging with a broad track and arriving at a ✖. Turn → and continue to a parking area beneath Cissbury Ring.

❹ Cross a farm road, go through a gate, follow the main bridleway track and climb around the **NE** flank of the hill fort. Go through a gate at the top of the track and continue for 200m to a ✖ above Deep Bottom. Turn → to descend around the head of Deep Bottom, then climb steeply and go through a gateway to a ✖ at the **S** of Cissbury Ring. Turn ← through a bridlegate and begin a 2km descent along a bridleway past Worthing and Hill Barn **golf courses**, before arriving at the A27. Turn → onto the westbound carriageway for 250m then turn ← to join the Findon–Worthing cycle route; follow the cycle route for 3km back to Worthing train station.

Signpost at Cissbury Ring

The long singletrack descent to Wepham Down

Route 14

Worthing – Springhead Hill Circuit

14

START/FINISH	Worthing train station TQ 146 034
DISTANCE	41km (25½ miles)
ON ROAD	9.5km (6 miles)
OFF ROAD	31.5km (19½ miles)
ASCENT	810m (2555ft)
GRADE	▲
TIME	3hrs–3hrs 30mins
PUB	The Frankland Arms at Washington
CAFÉ	Various in Worthing

75% OFF ROAD

Overview

This circular route traverses a sizeable area of the Downs north and east of Worthing. The route passes through some beautiful countryside taking in the Iron Age hill forts of Cissbury Ring and Chanctonbury Ring, as well as Downland ridges, coombes and woodland. There are fine views across the Downs, the Low Weald and the Channel coast. There are three major climbs: a steady 2km climb to Cissbury Ring from the A27; a steep climb from No Man's Land to New Hill along the Monarch's Way (MW); and a steep 1.5km pull up Highden Hill and Barnsfarm Hill from the A24, south of Washington. Several lesser climbs include short ascents over Barpham Hill and onto the flank of Church Hill. Most of the route follows well-maintained bridleways including several sections of the MW and the

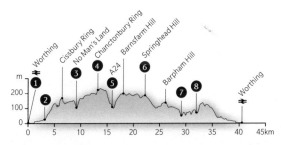

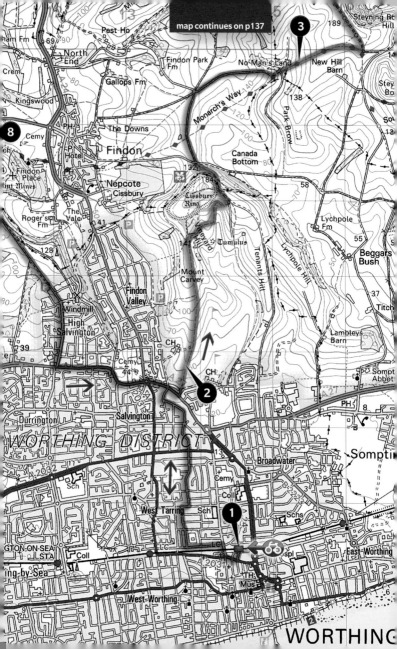
map continues on p137

South Downs Way (SDW). Conditions are generally good, although some bridle-ways can become muddy and churned up after wet weather. Watch out for horse riders and walkers, especially along the SDW.

Directions

1 From the station entrance follow the one-way street **S** for 150m to a **✕** with the **A2031**. Turn **→** then **→** again at a mini-roundabout, then **←** to follow the Worthing–Findon cycle route signs for 3km to arrive at a **✕** with the **A27**. Leave the cycle route here, turning **→** across to the farside lane and continuing **SE** along the **A27** for 250m then turning **←** off the road onto a bridleway (**there is no signpost**, although a plaque with the house-name *Skyring* is visible from the road).

2 Begin the long steady climb, initially on a tree-lined track, up through Hill Barn and Worthing **golf courses**, passing through a bridlegate onto the flank of **Cissbury Ring** after 2km. Turn **→** through a gateway at a **✕** and descend **NE**, skirting Deep Bottom, before climbing to a **✕**. Turn **←** and continue past the **NE** ramparts of the Iron Age hill fort before descending steeply to a gate. Continue **↑** over a **✕** and through a parking area. Continue **↑** over a

Climbing towards the ramparts of Cissbury Ring

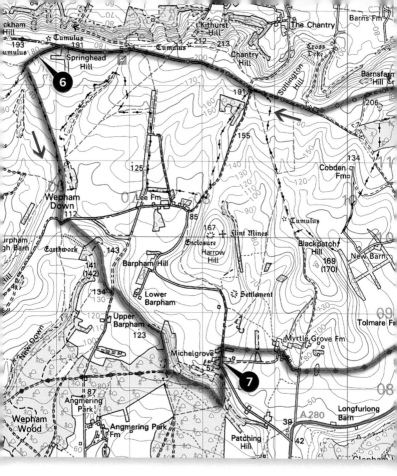

✖ then turn ➜ at the next ✖ and contour along a track before descending very steeply to a ✖ at **No Man's Land**.

③ Join the MW here, climbing steeply **NE** from No Man's Land for 1km on a track that was once a tarmacked road, before arriving at a ✖ with the SDW. Turn ← onto the SDW, climbing a little at first then continuing along the ridge. Take the **RH** fork after 2km then keep ↑ at the next ✖. Climb on a broad flint and grass track, cross a cattle grid and follow the track as it curves past the wooded Iron Age hill fort of **Chanctonbury Ring**.

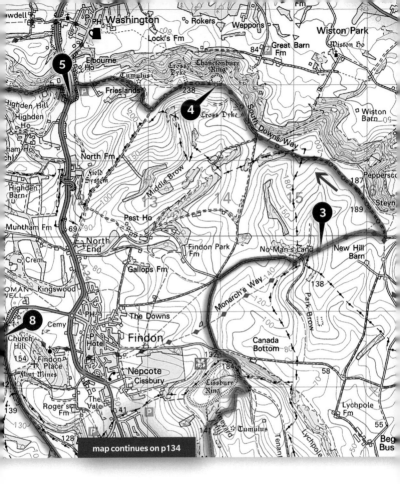

4 Continue along the flint and chalk bridleway, crossing a cattle grid then descending a little as the path begins to bend **SW**. Take a sharp **RH** turn to stay on the SDW and begin a steep 1.3km descent on a winding flint and chalk track. This is an excellent, exciting downhill, but **approach with caution**: the chalk has eroded into gullies criss-crossing the path, which is also strewn with sizeable flints. Coming off here – especially at speed – is going to hurt. Furthermore, you may well run into walkers, horse riders and mountain bikers coming the other way. As the gradient eases, pass straight

Heading north from Cissbury Ring to Chanctonbury Ring

through a car park and follow the track road as it leads around to the **left**.
Take care as you arrive at a slip road onto the A24. Cut across the slip road to
cross a grass bank on a tarmac path then cross the **S** and **N** lanes of the A24
via the central reservation at the obvious crossing point.

5 Once over, turn ← for a short way then follow a lane that leads to the **right**,
which turns **left** after 150m and begins to climb steeply **W** on a tree-lined,
tarmacked lane. Pass around a gate, emerging from woodland to continue
climbing the flank of **Highden Hill**. The gradient eases then climbs a
little over **Barnsfarm Hill**, passing through two gates before descending
through a third at a ✖. Continue over **Sullington Hill** and a ✖ at Chantry
Post car park (pass around gates either side) before crossing Kithurst Hill
and descending to pass the car park on the saddle between Kithurst Hill
and **Springhead Hill**. Continue along the ridge, passing through a copse
straddling the bridleway. On emerging from the copse, take the **LH** fork to
leave the SDW.

6 Descend steadily on the bridleway to a ✖ and turn ← then continue ↑ for
2km, losing then gaining a little height along the way. Pass through a gate
and continue ↑ over a ✖ before arriving at another ✖ shortly after. Turn ←
through a gate, continue for 100m then turn → through a gate and climb

the grassy slope of **Barpham Hill**, passing through a gate and continuing along the hilltop. Keep to the bridleway and as the path drops a little pass through a gate to a ✗. Turn ← then immediately bend → down a slope and go through a metal gate to follow the bridleway **SE** along the top of a steep escarpment. Go through a gate, enter the woodland of Michelgrove Park and continue to a ✗ (TQ 075 083). Turn ← to join the MW as it bends **SE**, then take the **LH** fork to stay on the MW. Continue along a section of bridleway, which **can be very muddy** after wet weather, before arriving at a ✗ (TQ 083 077). There is a signpost here with small arrows indicating the *MW*, although these are **easy to miss**. Turn ← off the main bridleway to continue on the MW. Descend the steep, wooded escarpment on a tricky chalk and flint track, emerging onto a country lane after 400m.

7 Turn ← and continue **N** along the lane, passing houses and paddocks. Pass by an automatic gate then turn → off the road onto a bridleway. Continue ↑ as the bridleway drops then climbs a little to arrive at **Myrtle Grove Farm** after 750m. Turn → through the farmyard and follow a minor road to a ✗. Dogleg ← then → through a gate to continue on the MW. Descend to a copse then climb over the flank of a hill, before passing through a gate and descending steeply down a rough, flinty track that **can be very muddy** after wet weather.

8 When the track bottoms out, climb steeply along the **RH** fork to the A280. Cross straight over the road – **beware fast-moving traffic** – and continue **S** along a bridleway on **Church Hill**. Keep ↑ for 2km as the track bends **SE** and descends steadily along Honeysuckle Lane to emerge on a road to the rear of **High Salvington**. Descend the road ↑ to arrive at a ✗ with the A27 after 900m. Turn ← onto the A27 and follow it **E** for 1.5km, ↑ over a roundabout (follow signs for *Brighton*), before dismounting to cross the road and joining the Worthing–Findon cycle route. Follow the *cycle route* signs for 3km to arrive at Worthing train station.

Tackling the steep ascent from Upwaltham

Route 15

Arundel – Graffham Down Circuit (and Amberley alternative)

START/FINISH	Arundel train station TQ 024 064 or Amberley train station TQ 026 118
DISTANCE	47.5km (29½ miles)
ON ROAD	5.5km (3½ miles)
OFF ROAD	42km (26 miles)
ALTERNATIVE	36km (22½ miles)
ON ROAD	2.5km (1½ miles)
OFF ROAD	33.5km (21 miles)
ASCENT	1125m (3685ft); alternative: 940m (3090ft)
GRADE	◆
TIME	4hrs–5hrs
PUB	Various in Arundel, The Bridge Inn at Amberley
CAFÉ	Various in Arundel, Riverside Café at Amberley

Overview

This is a long route that weaves its way around the Downs to the northwest of Arundel. Beginning in Arundel but with an alternative start at Amberley, much of the route follows bridleways through woodland 'hangers' and forestry plantations – it's

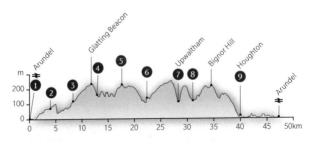

worth carrying a compass or GPS. As well as being an all-round excellent ride, this is a great route for a hot summer's day because of the shade. There are a number of noteworthy climbs: a very long, steady pull up from Fairmile Bottom along The Denture to Glatting Beacon; a short, very sharp climb up Barlavington Down; a long steady climb around the chalk quarry at Bishop's Ring to the South Downs Way (SDW); a long steady ascent on forest road and bridleway from Ripshook to Crown Tegleaze; a very steep climb up through farmland from Upwaltham; and a rolling climb on the Monarch's Way (MW) along the course of Stane Street Roman road to the SDW. The route is mostly on well-maintained bridleways and takes in sections of the MW, the SDW and even the West Sussex Literary Trail (WSLT). The longer main route includes a 1km section along the busy A29. After wet weather, some sections of the route are prone to churning up – in particular, the final section of the main route along the River Arun to Offham can be un-negotiable by bike in winter – a bail-out is included. Watch out and slow down for horse riders and walkers.

Ⓐ For the alternative start from Amberley train station, see page 146.

Directions

❶ Exit the train station, turning ⬅ onto the **A27** westbound. Keep ⬅ at the first roundabout to stay on the **A27**, cross the River Arun, take the second ⬅ (**A27**) off the next roundabout and pull into the layby. Wait for a gap in traffic – **this is a busy road** – and cross over to a minor road between two cottages. Continue past the cottages then turn ⬅ onto a bridleway and climb steadily through woods. The track levels out and bends **NW**, continuing along inside the edge of some woodland. On reaching an old wooden gate, the bridleway jinks **left** and continues through a metal gate and across a field to a second gate. Go through and continue along a track, ignoring a right-hand fork heading towards a trig point. Keep ⬆ as the track joins a minor road. Just before reaching **Rewell House**, take a **RH** fork off the main track onto a signposted bridleway.

❷ Continue through **Rewell Wood**, climbing a little and keeping ⬆ on a very straight forestry track, ignoring all intersecting paths until arriving at a signposted ✖. Take the **RH** fork of two tracks signposted as *bridleways* (blue arrows) and soon begin to descend the increasingly steep flinty path. Go through a gate, emerge from the woods and descend an escarpment. Go through a gate and down a slope to the **A29**. Turn ➡ onto the road,

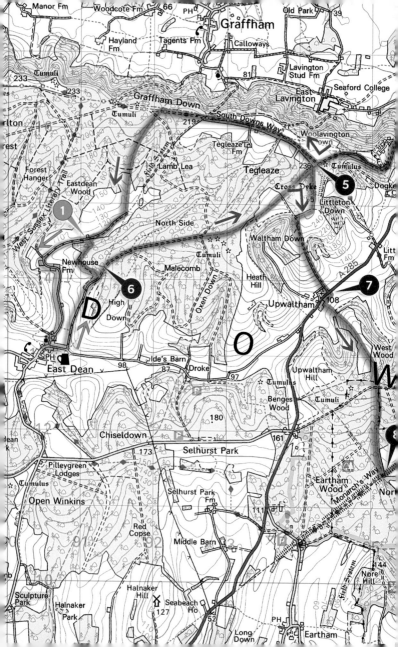

map continues on p142

crossing to the **NE**-bound carriageway and keeping to the edge of the road – **beware fast-moving traffic**. Continue **NE** for 1km to a layby, turn ← onto a bridleway, descend a short way then turn sharp → onto a singletrack path, which can be churned-up in winter. After 750m, the path bends sharp **left** and descends a short way before beginning a long steady climb through woodland, crossing a minor road en route. The path merges with the MW and continues **NW** along **The Denture**.

Alternative start/finish at Amberley train station

🅐 Exit the train station (TQ 026 118), turning ← onto the B2139, and head for **Houghton**. Pass through the hamlet then, as the road begins to climb beyond the George and Dragon pub,

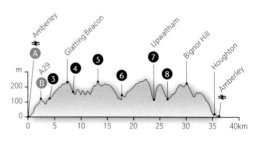

look out for a *bridleway* sign on the **RH** side of the road. Turn onto the bridleway, joining the MW; **take care as traffic can move fast** along this stretch. Climb steeply through woods on a narrow track, crossing ↑ over a private driveway, then continuing to climb along the edge of a field before the gradient eases and the path enters woods again. Continue ↑ along a wooded lane before the path climbs briefly, emerges from the woods and crosses fields to the A29.

🅑 Cross the road and continue ↑ to a signposted **LH** turn into **Houghton Forest**. Turn ← and continue to a ✖ then turn → along the MW. Continue ↑ as the path soon descends steadily, then keep ↑ over a ✖ as it climbs fairly steeply at length. The gradient eases and the alternative start now joins the main route.

⓷ Keep ↑ for the next 3km, ignoring all crossings until the twin masts on **Glatting Beacon** appear above and to the right. Turn → at the next ✖ to continue up a slight rise and cross over the SDW, continuing past the masts. Turn ← at a ✖ and go through a gate, then descend across a field to another

Heading for Barlavington Down

gate. Descend a steep, rutted chalk track **with caution**. Where the track levels, turn sharp → into the woods, ignore an immediate left-hand turn, then take the **LH** of three paths indicated by a rickety *signpost*.

4 Continue along a tree-lined track, across a coombe then around the flank of **Farm Hill**. Descend a chalk track through fields, continue ↑ along the edge of some woods, then tackle a very steep, rutted climb up **Barlavington Down**. At the top, continue ↑ over a ✕. The path then skirts the woods before descending steeply into woodland. Take the first sharp **LH** turn, mid-descent, then turn ← again and climb steadily on a bridleway, which is part of the WSLT. The bridleway exits the woods and descends across a field to the A285. Dogleg → then ← into a working quarry, turn ← and begin a long, steady climb up around and above the quarry. Ignore a right-hand fork and continue to a ✕ on the SDW at Crown Tegleaze.

5 Turn → along the SDW, continuing ↑ for 1.5km to a ✕ where the bridleway enters woods beyond **Graffham Down**. Turn ← (*East Dean*) and descend steeply through woodland, keeping ↑ over ✕s. Go through a gate and descend across meadowland to a ✕. Turn → onto a farm track and continue along the valley floor. Shortly before Postle's Barn, turn sharp ← at a bridleway signpost, go up a rise then turn → through a metal gate. Climb a little through woods, take the signposted **LH** turn and continue to a ✖ with a forestry road at Ripshook. Turn ← and climb steadily, initially on a forestry road.

Variant via East Dean

. . . .

1 Alternatively, from Postle's Barn you can continue along the valley on a farm track that becomes a road at Pond Barn and will lead you into the lovely village of **East Dean**, which has a pub among other attractions. To rejoin the route, head **E** out of the village on Droke's Lane and turn ← onto New Road bridleway.

. . . .

6 At a ✖ after 1.5km, keep ↑ on a bridleway, leaving the main forestry road. Continue, initially through woods, on a steady gradient then, just before reaching a ✖ with the SDW running along the ridge, turn → onto a bridleway (**no signpost**) and continue through woods. Where the bridleway emerges from the trees, turn → to descend a little then turn ← and descend steeply to **Upwaltham**, with its fine little 12th-century church. Keep ↑ and ignore the right-hand turn, unless you want to visit the church.

The tough climb up Barlavington Down

7 Go through a metal gate, cross a road and go through a wooden gate, then follow the bridleway that leads **right**, around to the rear of Upwaltham Farm. Turn ← through a metal gate (**no signpost**) and climb very steeply to another gate. Continue climbing steeply until the track levels and crosses fields. Enter the woods and descend a little over one ✗. At a second, dogleg → then ← to begin an excellent steep descent on flinty track through woods.

8 Arriving at a major ✗ turn sharp ← at a large wooden signpost indicating *Bignor*. Climb gently at first along the MW on **Stane Street** Roman road. **Beware tree roots** along this section. Keep ↑ to climb along Stane Street for 1.5km. Where the MW turns sharp right at a ✗ after passing through a gate, keep ↑. At the next ✗ turn → to join the SDW. Continue ↑ then turn ← and pass a parking area, turning → at a ✗ with a minor road. Climb a little over **Bignor Hill** then descend steeply, turning sharp ← at a ✗ before continuing to descend to another ✗ and turning → past some livestock sheds. Climb steadily, contour along for a while, then descend to the `A29`. Turn → along the edge of the road then cross over to continue on the SDW, descending steeply on a chalk and flint track to Houghton Lane. Turn → along the lane to a ✗ with the `B2139`.

Section **9** is not usually negotiable by bike in winter, so it may be best from here to retreat to Amberley, from where you can return to Arundel if that's where you started. To return to Amberley Station, turn ← out of Houghton Lane and continue along the `B2139` for 800m.

---

9 Dogleg → then ← onto South Lane. Descend the lane to a metal gate at the start of a bridleway and continue along a path following the meandering River Arun. The path **can be very muddy** and is **criss-crossed with tree roots** in places. The path also climbs away from the river before descending again several times. At **South Stoke**, dogleg ← then → across a road to rejoin the bridleway, which skirts the floodplain before climbing steeply past houses to join the road at **Offham**. Turn ← then immediately → to descend through a steep-sided cut before passing Arundel Wetlands wildfowl reserve and **Arundel Castle**. At the first roundabout, turn ← over a bridge and continue to a second roundabout, keeping ↑ to join the `A27` eastbound, arriving at Arundel train station shortly after.

Chalk track bridleway near Wepham Down

Route 16

Lancing – Amberley Mount Circuit

START/FINISH	Shoreham-by-Sea train station TQ 146 034 or Lancing Ring Nature Reserve TQ 183 063
DISTANCE	50.5km (31½ miles)
ON ROAD	5km (3 miles)
OFF ROAD	45.5km (28½ miles)
ASCENT	1090m (3580ft)
GRADE	◆
TIME	4hrs–5hrs
PUB	Various in Shoreham, The Gun and The Village House at Findon
CAFÉ	Various in Shoreham

90% OFF ROAD

Overview

This circular route starts at Shoreham, crosses the River Adur and takes to the hills by the grand edifice of Lancing College chapel. The route then swings west along the South Downs Way (SDW) above Worthing, almost as far as the Arun Valley, before returning via the Angmering and Michelgrove estates, Findon and Cissbury Ring. It takes in some beautiful countryside along Downland ridges, through coombes and woodlands. There are fine views across the Downs to the Low Weald and the Channel coast. There are four major climbs: a steady climb from Lancing

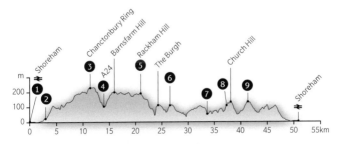

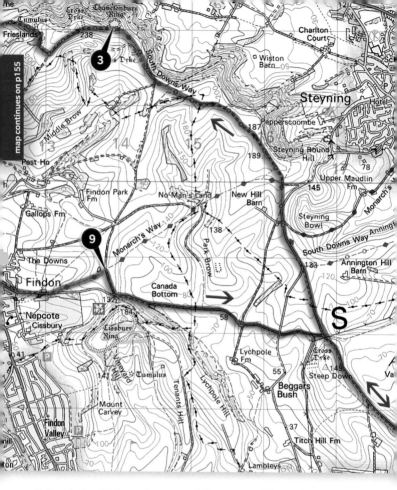

map continues on p155

College to the SDW over the course of 5km, a steep 1.5km pull up Highden Hill and Barnsfarm Hill from the A24, south of Washington, a very steep climb up to The Burgh from south of Amberley Mount and a steady climb to Cissbury Ring from Nepcote Green. There are several lesser climbs including a short pull up the flank of Church Hill. Most of the route follows well-maintained bridleways including several sections of the Monarch's Way (MW) and the SDW. Conditions are generally good, although some bridleways can become muddy and churned up after wet weather. Watch out for horse riders and walkers especially along the SDW.

Directions

1 From the station entrance, follow signs initially **W** on *Regional Cycle Route 79*. Turn **→** onto Old Shoreham Road at a mini-roundabout then turn **←** off the road to cross the River Adur via the Old Shoreham Bridge. Once across the Adur, continue **↑** to a **✕** with the `A27` at traffic lights. Turn **→** onto the **eastbound** carriageway of the `A27`, then immediately **←** onto Coombes Road. Take the next **←** then turn **→** to pass some houses and continue towards the cathedral-like edifice of Lancing College chapel, but fork **←** onto a bridleway before entering the college grounds.

> **A** There is a car park at the entrance to Lancing Ring Nature Reserve which could be used as an alternative start point.

2 Begin the long, steady climb up past Lancing Ring on a bridleway, with a section on tarmac, before emerging onto the Downs proper. Continue climbing steadily **NW (↑)**, passing through bridlegates and stock gates as you go. The bridleway intersects with the SDW 5km beyond the `A27`, and

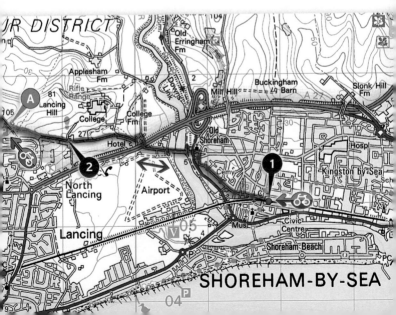

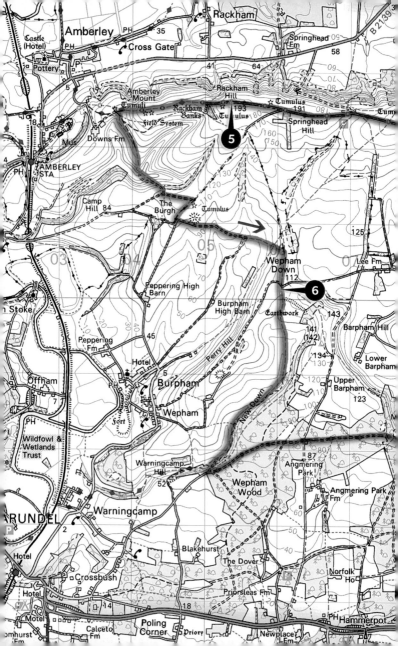

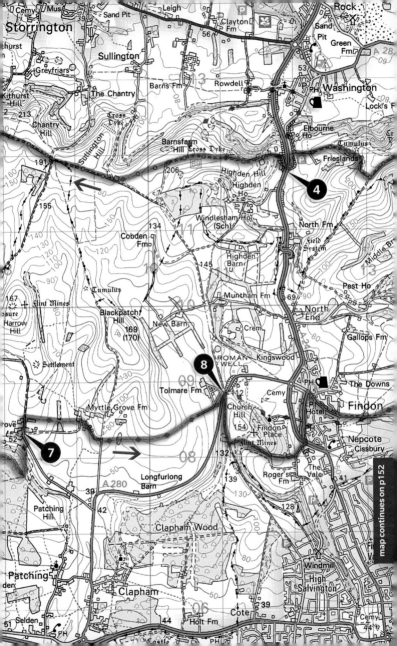

Storrington

Sullington

Greyfriars

The Chantry

Chantry Hill

Sullington Hill

Cobden Fm

Blackpatch Hill

New Barn

Harrow Hill

Settlement

Tolmare Fm

Myrtle Grove Fm

Longfurlong Barn

A 280

Patching Hill

Patching

Clapham

Selden

Clapham Wood

Holt Fm

Cote

Leigh

Clayton Fm

Barns Fm

Rowdell

Barnsfarm Hill Cross Dyke

Highden Hill

Highden Ho

Windlesham Ho (Sch)

Highden Barn

Muntham Fm

Crem

Kingswood

ROMAN WELL

Church Hill

Findon Place

Flint Mines

Rogers Fm

The Vale

Windmill

High Salvington

Rock

Sand Pit

Green Fm

Washington

Lock's

Elbourne Ho

Frieslands

North Fm

Field System

Pest Ho

North End

Gallops Fm

The Downs

Findon

Nepcote

Cissbury

map continues on p152

runs parallel to a minor road for 800m. Continue on the SDW as it crosses this road and climbs obliquely away from it at a bend. Keep ↑ over a ✕ and continue along the ridge. Take a RH fork after 2km then keep ↑ at the next ✕. Climb on a broad flint and grass track, cross a cattle grid and follow the track as it curves past the Iron Age hill fort of **Chanctonbury Ring**.

③ Continue along the flint and chalk bridleway, crossing a cattle grid then descending a little as the path begins to bend **SW**. Take a sharp **RH** turn to stay on the SDW and begin a steep 1.3km descent on a winding, flint-strewn chalk track. This is a great downhill, but the chalk has eroded into gullies criss-crossing the track, therefore **control your speed** – especially as you're likely to run into walkers, horse riders and mountain bikers coming the other way. As the gradient eases, pass straight through a car park and follow a track road that leads around to the **left**. **Take care** as you arrive at a slip road onto the A24. Cut across the slip road then cross the **S** and **N** lanes of the A24 via the central reservation at the obvious crossing point.

④ Once across, turn ← for a short way then follow a lane that leads to the **right**, which turns **left** after 150m and begins to climb steeply **W** on a tree-lined, tarmacked lane. Pass around a gate and emerge from woodland to continue climbing the flank of **Highden Hill**. The gradient eases then climbs a little over **Barnsfarm Hill**, passing through two gates before descending through a third at a ✕. Continue over **Sullington Hill** and a ✕ at Chantry Post car park (pass around gates either side) before crossing **Kithurst Hill** and descending to pass a car park on the saddle between Kithurst Hill and **Springhead Hill**. Continue along the ridge, passing through a copse

A perfect summer's day on Barnsfarm Hill

The long descent from Wepham Down

straddling the bridleway. On emerging from the copse, take the **RH** fork to stay on the SDW.

⑤ Continue over **Rackham Hill** and descend steadily by **Rackham Banks**. Go through a gate atop **Amberley Mount** and descend steeply. At a **✗** where the track levels, turn sharp **←** onto a broad chalk track byway. Fork **→** onto a bridleway after a short distance. Descend increasingly steep paths along field edges, arriving at a gate as the track bottoms out. Go through, cross the bottom of the coombe and climb a very long, very steep, flint-strewn track. At the top, go through a gate then turn **←** along a bridleway. At the next **✗** turn **→** then turn **←** again after 250m. Continue down and up along a bridleway before intersecting with another bridleway at **Wepham Down**. Turn **→** and continue **↑** to a metal gate with an *Angmering Estate* sign at a **✗**.

⑥ Go through and begin a long, steady, curving descent along the edge of a paddock running parallel to racehorse gallops. After the descent levels, continue along the valley floor, go through a gate, ignore the immediate left-hand path, continue to a fork and climb along the **LH** bridleway. Cross the first **✗** then turn **←** onto the MW, following an asphalted bridleway running **E** along the ridge through the woodland of **Angmering Park** then Michelgrove

Park. Continue ↑ as the asphalt eventually gives way to earth track. Continue ↑ and ignore a number of tracks criss-crossing the main bridleway until the track bends **SE** after 3km, then take the **LH** fork to stay on the MW. Continue along a section of bridleway, which **can be very muddy** after wet weather, before arriving at a ✖ (TQ 083 077). There is a signpost here with small arrows indicating the *MW*, but these are **easy to miss**. Turn ← off the main bridleway to continue on the MW. Descend a steep wooded escarpment on a tricky chalk and flint track, before emerging onto a minor road.

7 Turn ← and continue **N** along the lane, passing houses and paddocks. Pass around an automatic gate then turn → off the road onto a bridleway. Continue ↑ as the bridleway drops then climbs a little to arrive at **Myrtle Grove Farm**. Turn → through the farmyard and follow the lane to a ✖. Dogleg ← then → through a metal gate to continue on the MW. Descend to a copse then climb over the flank of a hill, before passing through a gate and descending steeply down a rough, flinty track that **can be very muddy** after wet weather. When the track bottoms out, take the **RH** fork to climb steeply to the A280.

8 Cross straight over the road – **beware fast-moving traffic** – continue **S** along the bridleway for 700m then take the **LH** fork. Descend steeply, bearing ← where the bridleway meets a concrete track. Descend to the A24, cross straight over and turn ← to a ✖ opposite a pub. Turn → and continue along the road through **Findon** village to a ✖ by shops and a post office. Turn → (*Cissbury Ring*) and follow a country road ↑ until it turns **left** opposite a green (again *Cissbury Ring*). Climb steadily along the road and turn ← onto a bridleway after passing houses. Climb steadily on a narrow path to a ✖.

9 Turn → and continue to a parking area beneath **Cissbury Ring**. Turn ← to descend on track and continue across country, up and down along byways and bridleways for 3km, keeping ↑ at all ✖s and crossing Titch Hill road before arriving at a ✖ below the **N** end of **Steep Down**. Turn → along a bridleway, gain a little height to Lancing Ring, then descend at length to join the road near Lancing College. Turn ← then → onto Coombes Road. Continue to a ✖ with the A27 at traffic lights, turn → onto the **westbound** carriageway then immediately ← at the next traffic lights to leave it again. Continue past Shoreham Airport, cross Old Shoreham Bridge, then turn → onto Old Shoreham Road then ← at a mini-roundabout, and retrace your outward route following Regional Cycle Route 79 to Shoreham-by-Sea train station.

Pedalling along lovely Standean Bottom (Route 17)

Blue skies in Castle Hill Nature Reserve

Route 17
Castle Hill Circuit

START/FINISH	Car park on B2123 Falmer Road TQ 356 063 or Brighton train station TQ 310 049
DISTANCE	16.5km (10 miles)
ON ROAD	750m (½ mile)
OFF ROAD	15.75km (9½ miles)
ASCENT	400m (1310ft)
GRADE	■
TIME	1hr 30mins
PUB	Numerous in Brighton, several in Rottingdean
CAFÉ	Numerous in Brighton, several in Rottingdean, Ovingdean Café

Overview

This superlative, short, sharp circuit is centred on Castle Hill on the Downs immediately
to the east of Brighton. There are two climbs
of note: a tough ascent up a steep-sided
coombe on a narrow path, immediately followed by a long, steep pull up to the South
Downs Way (SDW) at Swanborough Hill and

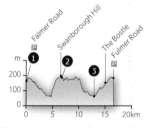

a short, steep ascent on a farm road followed by a long, steady climb over The
Bostle to the flank of Bullock Hill. There are also two excellent downhills: the end-
less, winding descent of an old drover's track along the side of Bullock Hill and
the precipitous descent from northeast of Newmarket Hill to Falmer Bottom on a
steep, flinty track. Conditions are generally good, even after wet weather. Watch
out for walkers and horse riders – particularly along the SDW sections.

Alternative start from Brighton train station

Ⓐ To get to the start of this route from Brighton train station, descend through
the tunnel under the station forecourt, heading **E** down Trafalgar Street for

200m before turning ← onto New England Road. Continue ↑ over traffic lights, join a section of cycle path ↑ before turning → at the next traffic lights and continuing for 200m to a ✗ at another set of traffic lights. Turn → and continue for 100m to traffic lights at the Preston Circus ✗. Continue ↑ over the traffic lights and ↑ again over another set after 300m. Continue for 1km along the A270 Upper Lewes Road to the Vogue Gyratory. Follow the gyratory around and take the second → turn, cross Lewes Road and climb very steeply up Bear Road for 1.5km. Turn ← at the top and continue along the Race Hill for 700m, turning ← off the road onto the Drove Road track at TQ 343 057. Continue for 1.5km, then cross the B2123 Falmer Road to arrive at the main start point. This adds 6km each way.

· ·

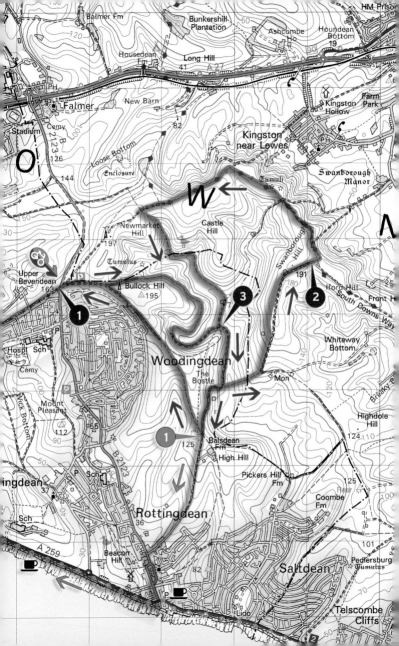

Directions

1 From the track next to the car park, take the **RH** fork, curving **E** above **Woodingdean**, then after 500m take the next **LH** fork. Contour around the **N** flank of **Bullock Hill**, go through a gate and begin the fantastic long, winding descent to arrive at Standean Bottom after 1.8km. Go through a gate and continue around to a **✕**. Take the second **RH** bridleway, which leads around the foot of the hill, bending **S** and passing through a gate. Continue **↑** on a steady gradient for 700m then, 50m before joining a farm road, turn sharp **←** off the main track through a gate onto a narrow path. Descend to the valley floor before climbing very steeply on a tough, bumpy path, passing through a gate near the top. Where the path levels out, turn **←** and continue to climb on a steep, even gradient for 800m. The track levels as you continue around the curving **S** ridge of **Swanborough Hill**, arriving at a dogleg **✕** with the SDW after 1.1km.

2 Go through the gate, turn **←** and continue **NW** along the ridge on the SDW, continuing **↑** over a **✕** after 1km. Pass through a gate and continue to a **✕** by some dew ponds. Turn **←** through the gate and continue **SW** along the Jugg's Road track, passing through a gate after 1km. Continue **↑** and, as the path starts to climb, turn **←** through a gate at **Castle Hill Nature Reserve**. Descend the steep, flinty track with due caution – **watch out for walkers and horse riders**. Just before the valley floor, pass through a gate, turn **←** and continue along Falmer Bottom beneath Castle Hill. Pass through a gate then make for another gate by some livestock sheds. Go through and continue **↑** to a **✕**.

Descending chalk track into Castle Hill Nature Reserve

3 Take the first **←** turn and follow the flinty track around to and through a gate, continuing **S** on

The high speed descent to Falmer Bottom

a slight gradient to a ✖ with a farm road. Go through a gate and turn ➔. Follow the road as it climbs quite steeply up out of the valley, by Balsdean Reservoir (130m). Just before the reservoir, turn ➔ off the road through a gate and soon continue to climb **NNW** on a steady gradient over **The Bostle**, skirting around **Woodingdean** on the **SW** flank of **Bullock Hill** and arriving back at the Falmer Road car park after 3km.

❶ For an alternative return route to Brighton from Balsdean Reservoir (9km), follow the route description of paragraph ❼ on Route 20 (page 186).

Climbing along the Sussex Border Path
to join the South Downs Way

Route 18
Brighton – Lewes Circuit

START/FINISH	Stanmer Park TQ 343 087
DISTANCE	29.5km (18½ miles)
ON ROAD	3km (2 miles)
OFF ROAD	26.5km (16½ miles)
ASCENT	640m (2105ft)
GRADE	▲
TIME	2hrs 30mins–3hrs
PUB	Numerous in Lewes – The Swan Inn is on route; The Swan Inn at Falmer
CAFÉ	Several in Lewes, Stanmer village

Overview

This challenging and varied ride takes in Downland ridges and woodland tracks and enjoys fine views across the Sussex Weald to the North Downs, along the Ouse Valley and over the English Channel between Brighton and Newhaven. The route is mostly on

bridleways and takes in sections of the South Downs Way (SDW). There are three major climbs: a steep, exceptionally tough ascent right at the start in Stanmer Park; a long steady climb to the SDW on grassy slopes; and a long, steep climb to Kingston Ridge on chalk track. Conditions are generally good, even after wet weather. Watch out for walkers and horse riders – particularly along the SDW sections.

There is a train station at Falmer adjacent to Stanmer Park and Sussex University, on the Brighton–Lewes line, although Stanmer Park is only a 5km ride from central Brighton.

The Chattri war memorial

Directions

1 Just inside the entrance to Stanmer Park, turn immediately ← along a track, making for a path that climbs very steeply into **Great Wood**. This is a **very tough climb** even in good conditions. At the top, continue ↑ over a ✖ and continue for 1.5km to pass a car park. Climb a little, keeping to the **LH** track, which soon bends **N**. Continue through woods to a ✖ with a farm road. Turn ← through a car park and onto a road. Jink ← and leave the road through a gate on the **right**. Descend across a field, through a gate and onto a track running parallel to the A27. Follow this for 2km to a ✖ with a farm road at TQ 303 096.

2 A waymarker pointing **N** indicates *Downs on your doorstep no. 40: Chattri & the Windmills*. Turn → through a gate and climb steadily on a grass slope. Pass through a gate after 1km, passing above the Chattri war memorial and then through another gate to continue on level ground (**prone to mud**) for 1km. Pass through a gate before the track climbs again to a ✖ with the SDW. Turn → to head **E** along the ridge on the SDW for 1.8km to **Ditchling Beacon** (248m).

3 Pass through a car park, cross a road, go through a gate and continue **E** along the gently-undulating ridge on the SDW, gaining and losing a little height along the way. After 2km, descend to a gate, pass through and cross a farm road **N** of **Streathill Farm** before climbing a little to **Plumpton Plain** on a broad chalk track. Continue along the level track for 1km before descending to a gate and a **✗**.

4 Pass **↑** through a gate (leaving the SDW) and follow the **RH** track along level ground to the **S** of **Blackcap** (206m). The track soon descends **SE** to a gate by some woodland. Go through and descend on a chalk track, which passes to the **left** of some stables and the old Lewes Racecourse after 1.5km. Continue to descend on a wooded singletrack path, **being alert for walkers and horse riders**.

5 The track bends **E** and passes HMP Lewes, before arriving at the `A275`. Turn **→** onto the road heading **S** to traffic lights at a **✗**. Continue **S** down the hill and bend sharp **←** at the bottom before climbing steeply to a mini-roundabout. Turn **→** along the `C7` road then immediately turn **→** onto a track road climbing gently **W** behind The Swan Inn. Turn sharply **←** across a bridge over the `A27`. Follow the track road as it bears **right** and climbs gradually past a few houses, paddocks and stables before levelling out. Pass through a gate and follow a track along a broad ridge for 1km, which passes to the **left** of a windmill and stables.

6 Go through another gate by some stables and descend past houses to **Kingston Hollow**. Cross the road, continue **↑** and climb on a gentle gradient past houses on a track road to arrive at a **✗** beneath Kingston Ridge. Continue **↑** and climb on a reasonable gradient along a chalk track to a gate. Go through and take the **LH** path. **This is a tough climb**: the track is very steep at first before easing off a little. At the top, turn **→** on the SDW heading **NW** along the ridge on level ground. After 700m, turn sharp **←** through a gate and climb to the top of a grassy slope on a steady gradient before descending to a gate.

7 Go through and turn **→** off the main track, continuing on the SDW. Continue to a gate and descend fairly steeply, passing through a gateway near the **S** corner of Newmarket Plantation. Turn **←** through a gate and dogleg **→** then **←** onto a bridleway that contours for 1km around the hillside to join the `B2123`. Turn **→** onto the road and descend for 1.6km, crossing the `A27` on a road bridge to arrive at a roundabout. Cross the roundabout **↑** then turn immediately **←** onto a cycle path. Descend for 1km past the entrance to **Sussex University** to arrive at the entrance to Stanmer Park.

Heading for Truleigh Hill on a rollercoaster chalk track

Route 19

Brighton – Truleigh Hill Circuit

19

START	Junction by the A27 at TQ 303 096 (park NE of Waterhall Roundabout TQ 302 096) or Brighton train station TQ 310 049
FINISH	Brighton Palace Pier TQ 313 039
DISTANCE	29.5km (18½ miles)
ON ROAD	5.5km (3½ miles)
OFF ROAD	24km (15 miles)
ASCENT	520m (1715ft)
GRADE	▲
TIME	3hrs–3hrs 30mins
PUB	Numerous in Brighton, Shoreham, Southwick Hove and Pyecombe; The Devil's Dyke Inn
CAFÉ	Numerous in Brighton; Hiker's Rest at Saddlescombe Farm

Overview

After a reasonably gentle start, this is a tough rollercoaster ride with many ups and downs including a couple of particularly challenging climbs. The route is mostly on bridleways, with some cycle path and road sections. The route takes in Downland ridges along one

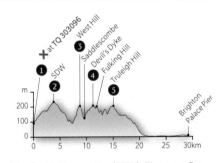

of the most spectacular sections of the South Downs Way (SDW). There are fine views north across the Sussex Weald to the North Downs, west to the Adur Valley and south to the English Channel between Brighton and Worthing. There are three major climbs: a long steady climb to the SDW on grassy slopes and across arable fields at the start of the ride; a long, steep climb to the top of West Hill – west of Pyecombe – on a chalk track; and a long climb – steep in its lower reaches – from Saddlescombe to the top of Devil's Dyke. Ground conditions are generally

ROUTE 19 BRIGHTON – TRULEIGH HILL CIRCUIT 173

map continues on p177

1

Scare
Hill

Tegdown
Hill

Sussex Border Path

Stanm

Waterhall

Patcham Place

Patcham

Schs

Red Hill

Westdene

D

Coldean

THE CITY OF
BRIGHTON AND HOVE

Hollingbury

Hollingbury
Castle

Moulseco

Mon
39

Roedale

Withdean

Coll Schs

Moulsecoo

Windmill

Mus

PRESTON PARK
STA

Hollingdean

Univ

Preston

Manor

Mus

Cemeteries

Crem

Coll

LONDON
ROAD STA

Coll

Hospl

A

Mus

Racecourse

White
Camp
Wh

HOVE

Mus

Law
Courts
Royal
Pavilion

College

Hospl

i360

West
Pier
(dis)

Mus's

Palace Pier

Brighton
Wheel
Aquarium

Kemp Town

Electric Rly

BRIGHTON

good, even after wet weather. Watch out for walkers and horse riders – particularly along the SDW sections.

Alternative start from Brighton train station

(A) To get to the start of the main route from Brighton train station, descend through the tunnel under the station forecourt, heading **E** down Trafalgar Street for 200m before turning ← onto New England Road. Continue ↑ over traffic lights to join a section of cycle path ↑ before turning → at the next set of traffic lights and continuing for 200m to another set of traffic lights at a ✖. Turn → at further lights, continue for 100m to traffic lights at Preston Circus ✖ and turn ← onto the A23. Continue **NW** along the A23 for 4km to Waterhall Roundabout. Turn first ← off the roundabout and continue under a railway bridge along Mill Lane. Turn → 100m after the bridge and go through the tunnel under the A27. Turn → and continue along the tarmacked lane as it bends **left** and climbs a little. After 600m, turn → and immediately → again to follow the track parallel to the railway line for 200m, before crossing the bridge over the A23. Continue ↑ to join a tarmacked lane, turn → and follow the lane, which bends **left** and soon climbs parallel to the A27 to arrive at a path ✖ at TQ 303 096.

Directions

(1) At the ✖ go through a gate with a waymarker pointing **N** and indicating *Downs on your doorstep no. 40: Chattri & the Windmills*. Climb steadily on a grassy slope, pass through a gate after 1km and continue above the **Chattri war memorial**. Pass through a gate as the track – **prone to mud after wet weather** – levels for 1km. Pass through another gate as the track climbs for 1km to a ✖ with the SDW.

(2) Turn ← and descend **W** along the ridge on the SDW for 1.5km to a ✖ **SE** of Jack and Jill windmills. Turn sharp ← through **New Barn Farm** on the SDW, then turn sharp → after 400m. Continue ↑ for 1km, passing **Pyecombe golf course** before crossing the A273 and turning ← onto a track running parallel to the road. After 200m, turn → and climb along a country lane to **Pyecombe Church** before descending to a slip road off the A23. Turn ← and cross the bridge over the A23. Turn ← to pass Haresdean Farm and turn → onto a bridleway (SDW). Pass through a gate and climb steeply to the top of West Hill – the **track is often churned-up** in its lower reaches – keeping → at a fork.

3 Pass through a gate at the top and descend a steep grassy slope towards Saddlescombe. This is a fast descent but **control your speed** as there is a drop-off, a fence and a gate near the bottom. Pass through a gate and descend along a sunken lane. Go through a gate and pass some houses and farm buildings at **Saddlescombe**. Turn ← down a slope and through a gate before crossing a road and turning ← through a gate onto a bridleway (SDW). Climb very steeply at first as the track bends **SW**, before settling into a gentler gradient. Climb for almost 2km before passing just **S** of **Devil's Dyke** (217m).

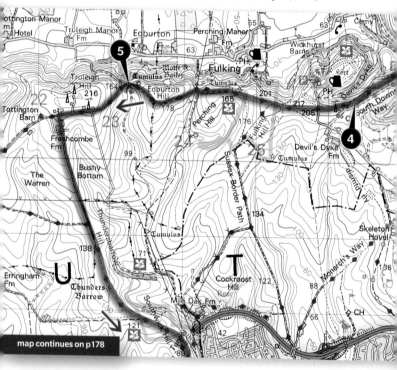

map continues on p178

4 Pass through a gate, cross Devil's Dyke Road and go through another gate to continue **W** along an obvious path for 700m. Pass through a gate and continue ↑ along the chalk track bridleway (SDW). The communications masts on Truleigh Hill are only 3km distant and look closer, but soon after

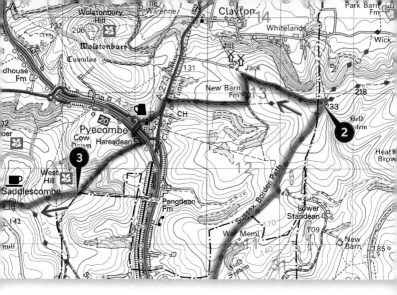

Devil's Dyke the SDW becomes a real rollercoaster ride. The track descends **W** of **Fulking Hill**, climbs a little then descends steeply to a **✕** between **Perching Hill** and **Edburton Hill**. Go through a gate and continue **↑** as the track climbs around Edburton Hill on a steady gradient. Passing **S** of the summit, the track descends in a long swoop to the saddle between Edburton Hill and **Truleigh Hill**. Go through a gate and climb steeply around to the **S** of Truleigh Hill summit. Near the top, the SDW becomes a potholed metalled track as it passes the communications masts.

Descending to Saddlescombe from West Hill

5 Turn next ← onto a bridleway through **Freshcombe Farm** and Summersdeane Farm. Descend for 1.5km, then go through a metal gate to join the Monarch's Way (MW). Continue ↑ as the track levels then rises a little over **Thundersbarrow Hill**. The track then bends **SE**, begins descending and passes through a gateway. Continue ↑ and pass through a gate, then continue descending ↑ on a chalk track along the MW. Go through a gateway, continue descending and then take the **RH** fork onto a byway (*purple arrow*). Descend along the byway to join a road and continue ↑ for 1.5km to pass under a railway bridge and then turn ← onto the A259. Continue past Shoreham Harbour, then follow signs for National Cycle Route 2 into Brighton.

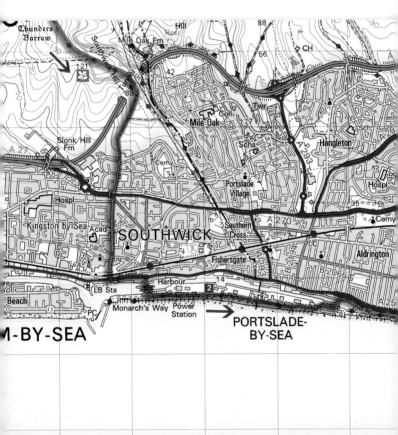

Climbing along Summer Down to Devil's Dyke

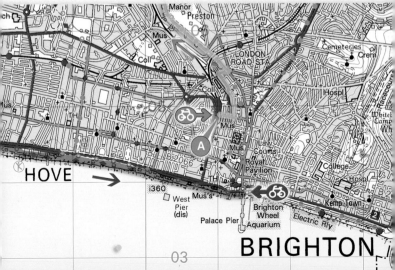

Climbing up Balmer Down from Ashcombe Bottom

Route 20

Devil's Dyke – Blackcap Circuit

START/FINISH	Brighton train station TQ 310 049
DISTANCE	44km (27½ miles)
ON ROAD	15km (9½ miles)
OFF ROAD	29km (18 miles)
ASCENT	990m (3240ft)
GRADE	▲
TIME	3hrs 30mins–4hrs
PUB	Numerous in Brighton and Rottingdean, The Devil's Dyke Inn, The Plough at Pyecombe
CAFÉ	Numerous in Brighton and Rottingdean, Hiker's Rest at Saddlescombe Farm

65%
OFF ROAD

Overview

This ride is a grand loop centred on Brighton, swinging around Devil's Dyke in the north-west, Blackcap in the northeast and finishing by coasting along

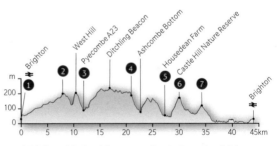

between Rottingdean and Brighton Marina. The route takes in Downland ridges, coombes and woodland tracks, with great views across the eastern Downs, across the Sussex Weald to the North Downs and down to the Channel coast. Aside from the 8.2km road section from Brighton station to Devil's Dyke at the start, the long on-road descent to Rottingdean and the cycle path/undercliff section from Rottingdean to Brighton at the end, the route is mostly on bridleways and takes in sections of the South Downs Way (SDW). As well as the road up to Devil's Dyke, there are four major climbs: a steep ascent of West Hill from Saddlescombe; a climb in stages from Ashcombe Bottom to Balmer Huff; a short, sharp climb, followed by a long steady pull up to Newmarket Hill from near the A27; and a steady climb on a farm road past Balsdean Reservoir. Conditions are generally good, even after wet weather. Watch out for walkers and horse riders – particularly along the SDW sections.

Directions

1 Exit the station to the **right** of the forecourt, turn **→** onto the A2010 and climb initially **N**, then bend **W** for 500m, turning **←** then **→** on the one-way system to arrive at Seven Dials Roundabout. Continue **↑** over it, then **NW** on the A2010 for 6.5km, keeping **↑** over traffic lights and roundabouts. At a **✗** by **Devil's Dyke Farm**, keep **↑** then bend **→** to arrive at a bridleway **✗** at TQ 258 107 after 200m.

2 Turn **→** onto the SDW and continue on a gentle descent along Summer Down. After 1km, the descent becomes ever steeper – **watch out for walkers and horse riders** – and bends sharply **left** before passing through a gate. Cross a road and continue **↑** through a gate, up a slope and then turn **→** along a track road through farm buildings and houses at **Saddlescombe**. Pass through a bridlegate and climb along a steepening sunken lane before passing through a gate. Continue **↑** and follow a fence up a steep grass slope before passing through a gate to the **S** of the summit of **West Hill** (211m). Continue **↑** on an initially gradual descent, which steepens considerably and descends a broad, rutted chalk track. Pass through a gate near the bottom of the descent and continue **↑** onto a farm road at Haresdean, which swings **left** onto a slip road, then turns **right** to cross the A23 on the SDW road bridge.

3 Once across, turn **→** off the slip road and climb past a church on a narrow lane. Keep **↑** at a **✗** and descend to the A273. Turn **←** and follow the path alongside the road for 200m, then cross the road and continue past

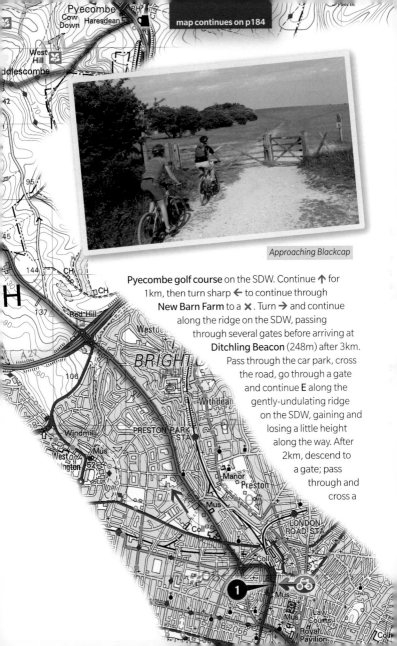

Approaching Blackcap

Pyecombe golf course on the SDW. Continue ↑ for 1km, then turn sharp ← to continue through **New Barn Farm** to a ✕. Turn → and continue along the ridge on the SDW, passing through several gates before arriving at **Ditchling Beacon (248m)** after 3km. Pass through the car park, cross the road, go through a gate and continue **E** along the gently-undulating ridge on the SDW, gaining and losing a little height along the way. After 2km, descend to a gate; pass through and cross a

map continues on p184

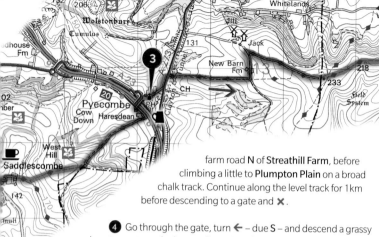

farm road **N** of **Streathill Farm**, before
climbing a little to **Plumpton Plain** on a broad
chalk track. Continue along the level track for 1km
before descending to a gate and ✖.

4 Go through the gate, turn ← – due **S** – and descend a grassy
slope to a gate set in the tree-line, which **isn't visible until you're
some way down the slope**. Pass through the gate and descend along a
bridleway **SE** through the woodland of **Ashcombe Bottom**. The path descends
steeply for 1km before levelling out. Continue ↑ as the path bends **S** along the
bottom of the coombe and emerges from the woodland. Go through a gate,
turn through the second **LH** gate at the next ✖ and climb a grassy slope **SW**,
passing through a copse as the gradient eases. Continue as the path bends
WNW on a steady gradient, soon arriving at a ✖. Turn → to pass through a
gate and continue **NW**, climbing steadily for 500m to a ✖. Go through a gate,
turn ← and continue along a chalk track, keeping ← at a fork. Climb a little
over Balmer Huff (170m) before descending, steadily at first (passing through

On Balmer Huff chalk track

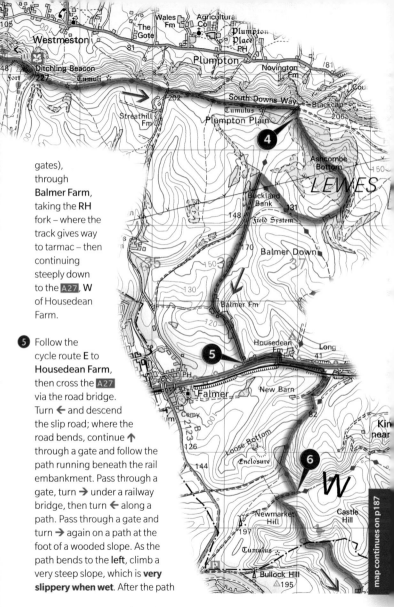

gates), through **Balmer Farm**, taking the **RH** fork – where the track gives way to tarmac – then continuing steeply down to the **A27**, **W** of Housedean Farm.

5 Follow the cycle route **E** to **Housedean Farm**, then cross the **A27** via the road bridge. Turn ← and descend the slip road; where the road bends, continue ↑ through a gate and follow the path running beneath the rail embankment. Pass through a gate, turn → under a railway bridge, then turn ← along a path. Pass through a gate and turn → again on a path at the foot of a wooded slope. As the path bends to the **left**, climb a very steep slope, which is **very slippery when wet**. After path

map continues on p187

levels, pass
through two
gates in quick
succession, then
continue ↑ on
a bridleway track,
climbing for 1km to
Newmarket Plantation,
passing through another
gate on the way. At a ✘ by the S
corner of Newmarket Plantation, turn
← through a gateway and continue climbing for
400m. Pass through a gate and continue to a ✘ on the
saddle **NE** of **Newmarket Hill**.

6 Turn → and, as the path climbs, turn ← through a gate at
Castle Hill Nature Reserve. Descend a steep, flinty track with caution –
watch out for walkers and horse riders. Where the path levels, turn ←
through a gate and continue along Falmer Bottom, beneath Castle Hill. Pass
through a gate then make for another gate by some livestock sheds. Go
through and continue ↑ for 250m to a ✘. Take the first ← turn and follow a
flinty track around to and through a gate, continuing **S** on a slight gradient
to a ✘ with a farm road. Go through a gate and turn → onto the farm
road. Follow the road as it climbs quite steeply up out of the valley, above
Balsdean Farm.

7 From the top of the ridge by Balsdean Reservoir (130m) descend for nearly
2km, initially on the farm road then on a residential street, to arrive at
the B2123. Turn ← and follow the road ↑ through **Rottingdean**, passing a
pond before arriving at a ✘. Turn ← along the High Street and continue to
the traffic lights at the ✘ with the A259. Turn → onto the A259 and join the
cycle path just beyond the bus stop. Continue **W** for 6km into Brighton.

Another option is to cross straight over the `A259` at Rottingdean and descend to the undercliff path. Turn ➔ – ride at a reasonable speed and **slow down** for others using the promenade – and continue along the undercliff for 4km to emerge on Marine Parade at the **W** end of Brighton Marina (if there is a diversion in place along the Brighton Marina section, climb to the clifftop route for this section). Continue along Marine Parade to arrive at a roundabout by Palace Pier and take the second exit for Brighton town centre and the railway station.

The sweeping descent from Swanborough Hill

21

Route 21

Brighton to Eastbourne

START	Stanmer Park TQ 343 087
FINISH	Eastbourne train station TV 610 991
DISTANCE	42.5km (26½ miles)
ON ROAD	35km (21¾ miles)
OFF ROAD	7.5km (4¾ miles)
ASCENT	985m (3235ft)
GRADE	▲
TIME	3hrs 30mins–4 hrs
PUB	Numerous in Brighton, Eastbourne and en route
CAFÉ	Numerous in Brighton and Eastbourne, Stanmer village, several in Alfriston

85%
OFF ROAD

Overview

This route is more than just a replication of the Brighton–Eastbourne leg of the South Downs Way (SDW) National Trail, as it includes extensive variants along the way. This is a fairly tough but glorious ride on varied terrain, including woodland tracks and Downland ridges, with relatively little on-road riding. There are fine views of the English Channel, across the Sussex Weald to the North Downs and across the Pevensey Levels. The route is mostly on bridleways and takes in sections of the SDW and Weald Way (WW). There are five major climbs: a long, steep, curving climb up Itford Hill on chalk track and grass slope; a long climb from the Cuckmere Valley to the Wilmington–Litlington Road on a steep, often slippery tree-lined track; a tough ascent on chalk track from Wilmington to The Holt; a long, steep climb from near Folkington to Teddard's Bottom; and the final, long climb from Jevington to the top of Bourne Hill. Conditions are generally good, although the woodland sections in particular can be very muddy after wet weather. Watch out for walkers and horse riders – particularly along the SDW sections.

There is a train station at Falmer, adjacent to Stanmer Park and Sussex University, on the Brighton–Lewes line, although Stanmer Park is only a 5km ride from central Brighton. Parking is available at Stanmer Park and Brighton University.

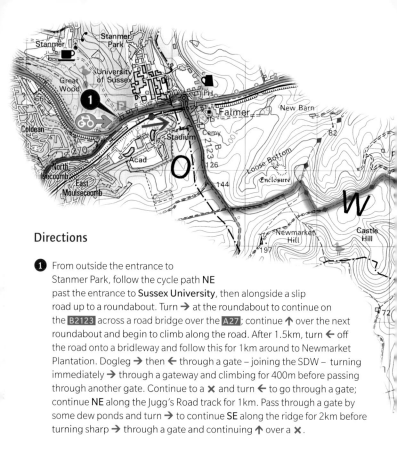

Directions

1 From outside the entrance to
Stanmer Park, follow the cycle path **NE**
past the entrance to **Sussex University**, then alongside a slip
road up to a roundabout. Turn → at the roundabout to continue on
the B2123 across a road bridge over the A27; continue ↑ over the next
roundabout and begin to climb along the road. After 1.5km, turn ← off
the road onto a bridleway and follow this for 1km around to Newmarket
Plantation. Dogleg → then ← through a gate – joining the SDW – turning
immediately → through a gateway and climbing for 400m before passing
through another gate. Continue to a ✗ and turn ← to go through a gate;
continue **NE** along the Jugg's Road track for 1km. Pass through a gate by
some dew ponds and turn → to continue **SE** along the ridge for 2km before
turning sharp → through a gate and continuing ↑ over a ✗.

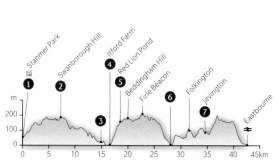

2 Continue **SW** along the bridleway track on **Swanborough Hill**, which bends **S** near a barn. Continue along the level track before descending steeply for 750m. Turn sharp **←** as the track levels and continue contouring, initially **E** bending to the **SE**, taking the **RH** turn when the path forks. Pass through two metal stock gates and two bridlegates located at regular intervals over the next 2.5km, before arriving at a **✗** near some houses. Turn **←** over a cattle grid and continue **SE** along a track to a **✗**. Turn **←** and descend steeply on the road through **Telscombe**, before climbing out the other side again. Cross the brow of the hill and leave the road on a bridleway track that leads to the **left**. Descend steeply for 400m, then turn sharp **←** to climb a little and pass through a gate. Turn **→** and descend until the track bottoms out, passing through a farm at Cricketing Bottom. Continue **↑** to rejoin the SDW. Continue **NE** for 1km along a track (**prone to mud**), then turn **→** just before the track reaches the **C7** road.

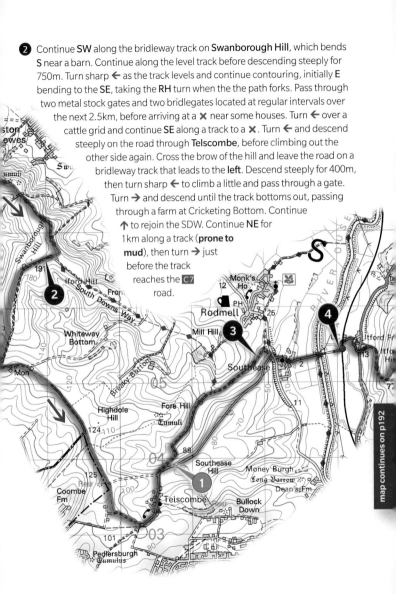

map continues on p192

On the Downs near Telscombe village

Variant after wet weather

1 This section can be very muddy after wet weather; staying on the Telscombe Road to the ✖ on the **C7** Lewes–Newhaven road is an option in this case.

3 Climb a little, pass through a gate and climb steeply a short way before descending through a gate to a road ✖. Dogleg ➔ then turn ⬅ down through Southease on a country road; cross the Ouse Valley and then the bridge over the River Ouse. Continue ⬆ then turn ⬅ then ➔ to pass over a railway level-crossing, through gates – **make sure the level-crossing lights indicate that it is safe to cross**.

4 Continue towards **Itford Farm**, turn ➔ (*SDW*) and follow the path across the bridge over the **A26**. Turn ➔ at a path ✖ and begin the long, winding climb up **Itford Hill**. The path initially climbs steeply **E**, then bends **S** and passes

On the ridge between Itford Hill and Beddingham Hill

map continues on p194

through
a gate; the
gradient eases, then
steepens once more as the path bends **E** again. Turn ← at a ✗ and climb **NE** on an ever-steepening grassy slope. The path bends **E** again near the top of the ridge. Continue on the SDW as the path trends **NE**, climbing a little and passing through a gate before reaching the summit trig point (164m) by **Red Lion Pond**.

5 Continue ↑ to a ✗ before reaching the communications towers on **Beddingham Hill**; cross a cattle grid and continue ↑ past the towers before descending steadily and passing through a gate after 1km. Cross a farm road and continue ↑ through a car park, exiting through a gate on the **left**. Continue along the ridge on the SDW, climbing gently for 1.5km

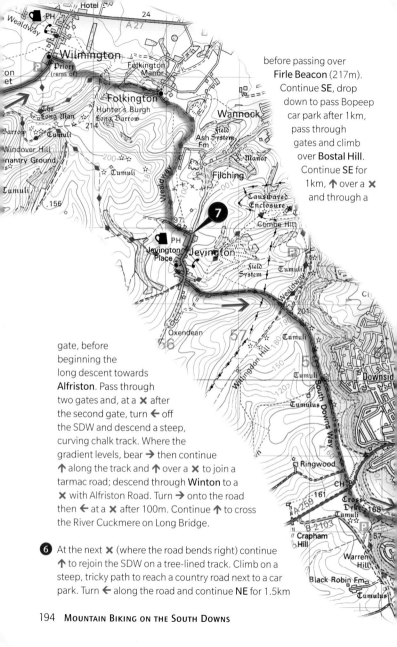

before passing over **Firle Beacon (217m)**. Continue **SE**, drop down to pass Bopeep car park after 1km, pass through gates and climb over **Bostal Hill**. Continue **SE** for 1km, ↑ over a ✖ and through a

gate, before beginning the long descent towards **Alfriston**. Pass through two gates and, at a ✖ after the second gate, turn ← off the SDW and descend a steep, curving chalk track. Where the gradient levels, bear → then continue ↑ along the track and ↑ over a ✖ to join a tarmac road; descend through **Winton** to a ✖ with Alfriston Road. Turn → onto the road then ← at a ✖ after 100m. Continue ↑ to cross the River Cuckmere on Long Bridge.

6 At the next ✖ (where the road bends right) continue ↑ to rejoin the SDW on a tree-lined track. Climb on a steep, tricky path to reach a country road next to a car park. Turn ← along the road and continue **NE** for 1.5km to **Wilmington** village, turning ➔ onto a track opposite the church. The track is initially level – and **can be very muddy in winter** – but it soon begins to climb, gradually at first then more steeply, to become a tricky chalk track, before it eases off and intersects with the WW. Continue through woodland along The Holt; the track contours for a while then descends to the rear of **Folkington** village. At the ✕ with the road through the village, keep ➔ and continue **SE** along the track. After 600m, the track bends **SW** and climbs for 1km, steeply at first, then more gradually to Teddard's Bottom before descending to a ✕. Turn ← and descend to a ✕ with Jevington Road.

7 Turn ➔ and continue for 750m through **Jevington**. Pass a dogleg ✕ after 650m and take the next ← onto the SDW. Begin the long, steady climb up the **W** spur of Bourne Hill, crossing the summit (201m) after 1.5km. Continue **SE** along the ridge on the SDW, looking down on Eastbourne to the **E**. Cross the **A259** after 2.5km and continue ↑ before taking the **LH** fork after 400m. Descend roughly **ESE** for 1km, initially on a grassy track, before arriving at the road by Paradise Plantation. Turn ➔ onto the road, bear ← after 300m and continue ↑ over the next ✕ before turning ← at a second ✕ after another 400m. Continue ↑ for 1km to a roundabout, then turn ➔ for the train station and town centre.

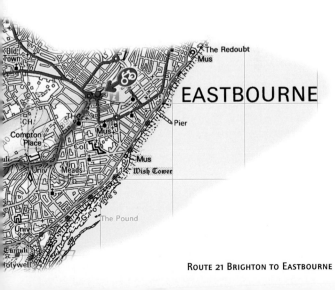

Climbing Western Brow near Ditchling Beacon

Route 22

Brighton – Ouse Valley Circuit

START/FINISH	Stanmer Park TQ 343 087
DISTANCE	43km (27 miles)
ON ROAD	6km (4 miles)
OFF ROAD	37km (23 miles)
ASCENT	990m (3240ft)
GRADE	◆
TIME	3hrs–4hrs
PUB	The Abergavenny Arms at Rodmell
CAFÉ	Stanmer Park

85% OFF ROAD

Overview

This is a challenging but hugely rewarding ride, taking in a variety of terrain including woodland tracks, Downland coombes and ridges. In clear conditions there are fine views of the Ouse Valley, the English Channel between Brighton and Newhaven and across the Sussex Weald to the North Downs. There are six major climbs: a steep, difficult ascent right at the start in Stanmer Park; a short, sharp up and down, followed by a long, steady climb to the South Downs Way (SDW) by Ditchling Beacon; a steep, difficult climb through woodland at Bunkershill Plantation; a short, sharp then long even-gradiented pull up to the SDW by Newmarket Hill; a tough, steep climb up a shrub-covered escarpment from Dean's Farm to Bullock Down; and a long, winding climb around Bullock Hill on an old drover's track. The route is mostly on bridleways and takes in sections of the SDW. Conditions are generally good, although the woodland sections in particular can be fearsomely muddy after wet weather. Watch out for walkers and horse riders – particularly along the SDW sections.

There is a train station at Falmer adjacent to Stanmer Park and Sussex University, on the Brighton–Lewes line, although Stanmer Park is only a 5km ride from central Brighton.

Directions

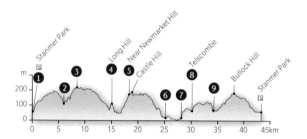

1 Just inside the entrance to Stanmer Park, turn immediately ← along a track for 300m, making for the track that climbs very steeply into Great Wood. This is an **exceptionally tough climb** even in good conditions. At the top, continue straight over a ✗ and follow a track ↑ bearing **NW** for 1.5km to a car park. Climb a little, keeping to the **LH** track, which soon bends **N**. Continue through the woods to a ✗ with a farm road. Cross the road and pass around a barrier onto a track continuing **N**, still through woodland. Pass through a gate, jink ← through an opening in a fence and continue **N** across a level, grassy field for 1km to a gate into a wooded area. Climb a little on a steady gradient, before turning → at the top, descending a little and continuing ↑ to a ✗. Turn → and descend steadily for 1.5km to a ✗. Turn ← to descend through woodland, passing through a gate at the bottom.

2 Continue ↑ on a bridleway, pass through a gate and follow the path around the foot of Bow Hill, before a short, steep climb to a ✗. Go through a gate, turn ← and descend, passing through another gate before reaching the bottom. Climb, fairly steeply at first, pass through a gate and continue to climb steeply for 1km, before passing through a gate and turning → then → again to continue **E** along the gently undulating ridge on the SDW, gaining and losing a little height along the way.

3 After 1.5km, descend to a gate, pass through and cross a farm road **N** of Streathill Farm before climbing a little to Plumpton Plain on a broad chalk track. Continue along the level track for 1km before descending to a gate and a ✗. Don't go through; instead turn → on the SDW and continue on a slight descent for 1km to a ✗. Turn ← on the SDW and descend for nearly 2km, passing through two gates, before arriving at a ✗. Turn → through a gate, continuing on the SDW, and descend along a path **pot-holed by**

rabbit burrows. The path bottoms out then begins to climb in an inverted S-curve through **Bunkershill Plantation**. This is a short, tough climb, which is slippery after rain. Continue through woodland, emerging on the brow of **Long Hill**.

4 Descend the steep hillside with care, slowing down before approaching the gate at the bottom. Pass through the gate, descend several steps, turn → onto the Lewes–Brighton cycle path and follow it past **Housedean Farm** before forking ← onto a slip road then crossing a bridge over the A27. Once across, turn ← and descend the slip road. Where the road bends, continue ↑ through a gate and follow the path beneath the railway embankment. Pass through a gate, turn → under a railway bridge then ← along a path. Pass through a gate and turn → again on a path at the foot of a wooded slope. As the path bends **left**, climb a very steep slope, which is **slippery when wet**. After the path levels, pass through two gates in quick succession, continue ↑ onto a track and climb for 1km to Newmarket Plantation, passing through another gate on the way. At the ✖ by the **S** corner of the plantation turn ← through a gateway and continue climbing for 400m. Pass through a gate and continue to a ✖ on the saddle **NE** of **Newmarket Hill**.

5 Turn ← on the SDW, pass through a gate and continue **NE** along the Jugg's Road track for 1km. Pass through a gate by dew ponds and turn → to continue **SE** along a ridge path for 2km, before turning sharp → through a gate and continuing a short way to a ✖. Turn ← onto a concrete farm track and descend for 1.5km, passing over two cattle grids. Cross the farm road and pass through a gate. Continue descending on the path and pass through gates either side of another farm road to continue on a gentle incline. Pass through a gate and continue along a fence- and shrub-lined path to a ✖. Pass through a gate (*SDW*), descend a steep bumpy track and pass through a gate. Turn ← then, after 50m, ← again.

6 Continue **NE** for 1km along a track (**prone to mud**), then turn → before the track reaches the C7 road. Climb a little, pass through a gate and climb steeply a short way before descending through a gate to a road ✖. Turn → along the C7 and continue for 2km, then turn → onto a farm road at **Dean's Farm**. Bear ← and pass around a large wrought iron gate, continue along a farm road for 600m, then turn → off the road onto a bridleway through a gap between a hedgerow and a stock fence. Continue along a field edge beside the hedgerow for 100m, then make for a bridlegate diagonally across the field and up a slight rise.

7 Go through the gate and climb steeply up an escarpment through shrubbery and bushes on chalk track (these **can be overgrown** in summer). Pass through a gate shortly before the escarpment levels out, then bear ← and make for the obvious bridlegate. Pass through and continue on a narrow bridleway before emerging onto a concrete track road. Continue ↑ for 800m, passing houses along Bullock Down, before leaving the track road where it bends **SW**, keeping ↑ and descending along a wooded bridleway – **watch out for tree roots** – before arriving in **Telscombe** village.

8 Turn ← onto a country road by the YHA and climb steeply out of the village. At the brow of the hill, turn first → at a ✕ to continue for 500m along a bridleway. Cross a cattle grid then turn → to go through a bridlegate and continue **N**. Follow a bridleway along the ridge, passing through another bridlegate and two metal stock gates, as the path trends **NW** for 2.5km before bending **W**. Bear ← at a fork to drop down through a gate, then descend steeply on a narrow bumpy path to the valley floor before climbing a little and passing through a gate at a ✕.

9 Turn → and continue **N** on a steadily descending chalk track for 750m. Pass through a gate as the path bends **left** and arrives at a ✕. Turn second ← and follow the track as it curves around Standean Bottom at the foot of the escarpment, passing through a gate. The path loops around and begins to ascend initially **NE**, then curves to climb

Descending the grassy track on Bullock Hill

around the flank of **Bullock Hill** on a steady gradient for 1.5km. Pass through a gate where the path levels out and continue to where the path converges with another bridleway. Continue ↑ and descend **W** to the `B2123` Falmer Road. Turn → onto the road and descend for 3km, crossing the `A27` on the road bridge before arriving at a roundabout. Cross the roundabout ↑ then turn immediately ← onto the cycle path. Descend for 1km past the entrance to Sussex University before arriving at the entrance to Stanmer Park.

Sinuous chalk track on Lullington Heath (Route 23)

Routes around Eastbourne

Descending into Friston Forest near Winchester's Pond

Route 23

Friston Forest Circuit

START/FINISH	Seaford train station **TV 482 992** or Exceat car park **TV 518 996**
DISTANCE	22km (13¾ miles); 14.5km (9 miles) if starting at Exceat
ON ROAD	8km (5 miles)
OFF ROAD	14km (8¾ miles)
ASCENT	510m (1675ft)
GRADE	■
TIME	2hrs; 1hr 30mins if starting at Exceat
PUB	Various in Seaford, The Golden Galleon near Exceat, The Eight Bells at Jevington
CAFÉ	Various in Seaford, café near Exceat visitor centre

Overview

Friston Forest is a fairly short (under 4km) and agreeable ride from Seaford train station; otherwise there is a car park at Exceat. There are several dedicated, colour-coded MTB routes around Friston Forest with plenty of singletrack and a

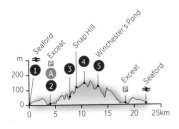

purpose-built downhill route. Hours of improvised fun can be had around Friston Forest, but the route described here is more of a circuit around the forest. This is a short, sweet woodland ride with fine views of the eastern Downs and the Channel from Lullington Heath. There are a few ups and downs with two major climbs: a steady climb over Snap Hill and a steeper ascent of Jevington Holt. Conditions are generally good but the track running along the east flank of the forest can be very muddy in winter, especially the section down through woodland to Jevington Holt. A variant route via Jevington is provided if this is the case, which adds a further 1.5km distance and 65m ascent.

Directions

1 From the station entrance, turn → and cross a mini-roundabout, then continue through Seaford on the `A259` for 2.5km before emerging from the eastern end of the town overlooking the Cuckmere Valley. Descend for 1km to **Exceat Bridge**, cross the Cuckmere River and arrive at a ✖ after 500m. Turn ← then → (*Seven Sisters Country Park*) for Exceat car park at TV 558 916 at the **SW** corner of **Friston Forest**.

> **A** If driving, Exceat car park is a good alternative start/finish point.

2 Turn ← on a bridleway before the parking area and continue beneath the **NW** spur of Exceat Hill for 850m to a ✖ by Westdean Pond. Go through a gateway and turn ← then first → to continue through the hamlet. Keep ↑ at the next ✖ and climb steeply **E** on a tarmacked forest track. The path soon levels out and the tarmac gives way to gravel. At the next fork, take the **RH** turn up a slight rise and continue **SE**. After 800m, leave the gravel track, keeping ↑ as it bends to the left. Descend ↑ to cross over a forest track and then climb steadily along the flank of **Friston Hill**. The path levels and emerges from the woodland at the **SW** end of a gallops, before descending to a ✖ near **Friston Place** at TV 547 989. Turn ← and then, after 175m, ← again at the next ✖.

3 Climb a short distance through trees before crossing over the gallops on Friston Hill – be aware that **horses may be being exercised here** – and into Friston Forest on the far side. Continue along bridleway, which is **prone to mud** in winter, descending to a ✖ after 500m. Continue ↑ to climb steadily up and

over **Snap Hill**. The track levels out over Long Brow and at a ✖ (TV 545 005), where the track begins to descend, turn ➔ and continue on a slight gradient above a steep escarpment, crossing a forest track shortly before emerging from the forest and, after 1km, reaching a ✖ at TQ 554 009. Turn immediately ⬅ if the path isn't too muddy, otherwise use the variant route described below.

Variant route from ✖ at TQ 554 009

① From the ✖ continue ⬆ steeply downhill on a rutted chalk track to the **NE**. As the gradient lessens, continue ⬆ over a ✖ and soon pass around a gate to emerge at Jevington Road after 1km. Turn ⬅ and continue along Jevington Road for 700m, then turn ⬅ onto a track road at TQ 564 019. Continue ⬆ on a gentle climb and keep ⬅ at a fork before the path swings **SW** and climbs more steeply. Pass two ✖s and rejoin the main route, intersecting briefly with the South Downs Way (SDW) as the path curves steeply up through woodland at Jevington Holt to arrive at a ✖ at the top of the climb.

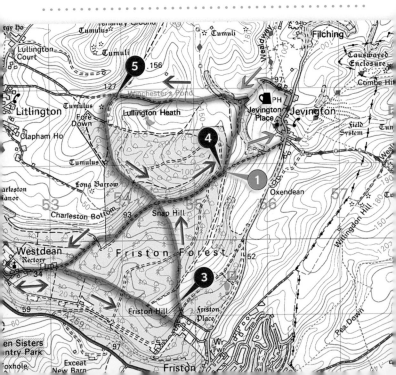

Steep drop-off in Friston Forest

4 Continue along the forest edge for 450m then take the **RH** fork, go through a gate and descend a little into woodland (this path **can be totally churned up in winter or after wet weather**). Continue descending gradually, arriving at a ✗ after 500m. Turn ← onto the SDW, then keep ← at the next ✗ shortly after. Climb briefly but steeply up through the wooded flank of Jevington Holt to arrive at a ✗ at the top.

> Variant **1** rejoins the main route here.

Leave the SDW and continue ↑ through a gate onto **Lullington Heath Nature Reserve**, dropping into Old Kiln Bottom, before climbing a little to a ✗ at **Winchester's Pond**.

5 Turn ← (**SW**), following a bridleway that soon enters woodland, bending **S** then **SE** and descending fairly steeply for 1km. At the bottom of the descent, turn second → at the ✗ to continue ↑ and climb **SE** (this is a complex ✗ – **check the map**). At a fork, keep → and continue climbing steeply up **Snap Hill** to a ✗ just below Long Brow. Turn → and contour **SW** for 750m, then fork → and soon begin descending – keep ← at the next fork – for 1.5km into **Westdean**. Retrace your outward route through the village, past the pond and around the **NW** spur of Exceat Hill to arrive back at the Exceat car park. To return to Seaford, retrace your outward route.

Climbing along The Comp track, with the English Channel in the background

Route 24

Seaford – Firle Beacon Circuit

24

START/FINISH	Seaford train station TV 482 992
DISTANCE	28.5km (17¾ miles)
ON ROAD	7.5km (4¾ miles)
OFF ROAD	21km (13 miles)
ASCENT	520m (1700ft)
GRADE	■
TIME	2hrs–2hrs 30mins
PUB	Various in Seaford; The Ram at Firle
CAFÉ	Various in Seaford; Charleston Farmhouse near Firle

75%
OFF ROAD

Overview

This is one of the easier routes in this guidebook, but it makes for a really enjoyable ride and covers a lot of distance fairly rapidly. There are good views of the Cuckmere Valley, the Channel and the Weald, along with the gentle southern

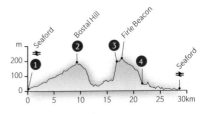

slopes and the steep northern escarpment along this stretch of the Downs. The route is mostly on bridleways and takes in sections of the South Downs Way (SDW). There is a 2.5km road section through Seaford at the beginning and 4.5km from Norton to Seaford station at the end. Excluding the gradual climb up to the main ridge of the Downs north of Seaford, there is only one major climb on this route, but it's a killer: a 1km climb on an often hoof-damaged path traversing the steep northeast escarpment of the Downs south of Charleston Farmhouse. Except parts of The Comp track between the Alfriston Road and Bopeep and the Comp Lane track from Winton to Charleston, which are prone to mud in winter, conditions are generally good. Watch out for walkers and horse riders – particularly along the SDW sections.

map continues on p213

Directions

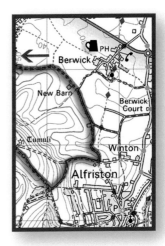

1 From the station entrance, turn → and cross the mini-roundabout, then continue through Seaford on the **A259** for 2.5km. Just before reaching the town's **E** extremity, turn ← onto Chyngton Lane North at TV 504 994. Continue ↑ to pass the turning for the farm and continue ↑ along the bridleway. Cross the Alfriston Road after 1km. Climb gently for 1km to Camp Hill (90m) and continue along **The Comp** track, climbing very gradually in a broad arc for 4.5km, and passing through a few gates en route, before arriving at the top of the ridge. Go through a gate and turn → onto the SDW, passing through two gates to the rear of the car park at Bopeep and climb briefly over Bostal Hill.

On Firle Beacon, with Mount Caburn and Lewes in the background

Beginning the long descent to the Cuckmere Valley

2 Continue **SE** along the ridge, descending past a **✗** and passing through a gate. Descend a flinty track for 1.2km to a **✗** then turn **←** and descend along a chalk track. Keep **←** at a fork and continue steeply downhill, bending **E** as the track bottoms out then continuing **↑** to a **✗**. Turn **←** then take the **LH** fork to continue along the Comp Lane track. Descend, then climb a little past Comp Barn. Contour along with minor ups and downs beneath the northern escarpment of the Downs, keeping **↑** at all **✗**s for 3.5km, before arriving at a **✗** at TQ 492 062. Turn **←** and begin to climb, steadily at first, towards the steep **NE** escarpment of the ridge. Pass through a gate where the **often hoof-damaged** path becomes **very steep** as it traverses **S** across the face of the escarpment.

3 Arrive on the ridge after 1km, turn **→** onto the SDW and continue **NW** along the ridge to cross **Firle Beacon** (217m), then descend gently **W**, passing through three gates before arriving at a car park after 2.5km. Pass through

the car park then turn ← at a ✖ to descend on a farm road, passing through **Blackcap Farm** – **slow down through the farm yard** – and exiting through a gate at TQ 466 051. Continue ↑ across a grassy field, pass through a gate and descend steeply – initially on a track – to pass through another gate. Continue downhill for another 1km.

4 Pass through a gate and continue along Stump Bottom. Arrive at a ✖ after 900m, turn → and climb steadily for 300m to a ✖. Turn ← and descend along the track, steeply at first, before continuing along **Poverty Bottom** to **Norton**. Continue on a country road winding through Norton and **Bishopstone** for 2km to reach the A259. Turn ← along the A259, then turn → after 200m, continuing under a railway bridge. The road soon bends **left** and continues along Seaford seafront. After 1.2km, turn ← off the seafront road at a mini-roundabout. Continue ↑ for 400m, then turn ← and ← again to arrive at Seaford train station.

Windover Hill with the Cuckmere Valley beyond

Route 25

Eastbourne – Cuckmere Valley Circuit

START/FINISH	Eastbourne train station TV 610 991
DISTANCE	34km (21 miles)
ON ROAD	7km (4½ miles)
OFF ROAD	27km (16½ miles)
ASCENT	815m (2675ft)
GRADE	▲
TIME	2hrs–3hrs
PUB	Various in Eastbourne, The Plough and Harrow at Litlington, The Eight Bells at Jevington
CAFÉ	Various in Eastbourne, Litlington Tea Gardens

Overview

This route loops around the Downs west of Eastbourne, between Bourne Hill and the Cuckmere Valley, taking in chalk ridges, woodland tracks and Downland villages, while benefiting from great views across the

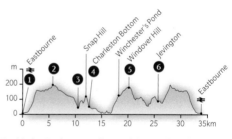

Pevensey Levels, the Sussex Weald, the Cuckmere Valley and the English Channel. The route is mostly on bridleways with a few short road sections and takes in sections of the South Downs Way (SDW) and the Weald Way (WW). There are four major climbs: 1km on path and grassy slope from Paradise Plantation to Warren Hill at the start; a long steady climb over Snap Hill in Friston Forest; a steady 3.5km climb to the top of Windover Hill from Litlington via Winchester's Pond and the final pull over Bourne Hill from Jevington. Except the section through Friston Forest, which is prone to mud in winter, conditions are generally good. Watch out for walkers and horse riders – particularly along the SDW and WW sections.

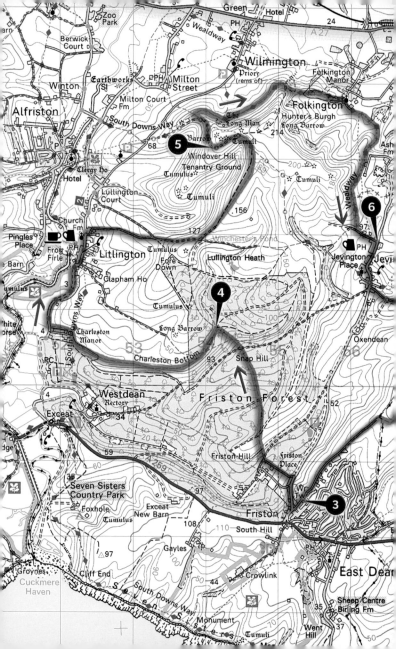

Directions

By Winchester's Pond

1 From the station entrance, turn → and → again, arriving at a roundabout after 100m. Take the first ← turn (*Beachy Head*) and continue ↑ to pass the Law Courts and some playing fields, keeping → then → again at a ✕ after 1km. Continue ↑ for 400m, going over a ✕ then taking the **RH** fork, before arriving at Paradise Plantation after 300m. Turn ← onto a bridleway path. Climb **WNW** for 1km, initially on a path then on a grassy track. Continue ↑ at a ✕ just **NW** of a trig point (joining the SDW), crossing the A259 after 400m. Continue **NW** for 2.5km, gaining a little height and going over a ✕ before the summit of Bourne Hill (201m).

2 Continue ↑ for 100m to the next ✕ then turn ← onto a bridleway track running along the ridge of **Willingdon Hill**, descending gently for almost 2km before the track turns sharply **right**. Ignore the first gate on the left, then take the **LH** turn through a gateway to continue **SW** along the Friston Dencher track, which becomes tarmac road as it passes large detached houses on the **left** and arrives at a ✕ after 1.7km. Turn sharp → and continue along the road for 400m, taking the second ← (a private road, but with a *public bridleway* signpost) and descending the track road past **Friston Place**.

3 At the next ✕ take the second → turn to climb **NW** through trees before crossing the gallops on **Friston Hill** – be aware that **horses may be being exercised here** – and continuing into **Friston Forest** on the far side. Continue along the bridleway, which is **prone to mud in winter**, descending to a ✕ after 500m. Continue ↑ and climb steadily up and over **Snap Hill**. Continue ↑ over a ✕ after the track levels out over Long Brow and descend precipitously to Charleston Bottom – keeping → where the path forks halfway down.

4 Arriving at the confluence of paths at the bottom of the hill, turn sharp ← and continue along **Charleston Bottom** for 2.75km, skirting around the grounds of **Charleston Manor**, before emerging directly onto the Litlington Road. Turn → and continue along the winding country road for 1.5km through **Litlington** village, then turn ➜ just past and opposite the church. Turn ← through a farmyard, then ➜ again and begin to climb **E** along the flint and chalk bridleway, arriving at a ✖ by **Winchester's Pond** after 1.5km. Take the **LH** path and soon begin climbing steadily, initially **NE** then bending **NW** in a broad sweep, passing through three gates before reaching the top of **Windover Hill** (188m) after 2km.

5 Continue ⬆ and begin the hugely enjoyable curving descent on an excellent flint and chalk track, but **keep to a sensible speed** – slow down and give way to other users. Halfway down, as the track begins to bend **SW**, fork ➜ where the path appears to double up at **TQ 539 035** and continue ⬆ to descend for 100m before turning sharp ➜ at a ✖. Go through the gate, descend a little then contour along beneath the steep **N** escarpment and the **Long Man of Wilmington** for 1.4km. The path climbs a little and as it swings **E** around the flank of the hill go through a gate and turn ➜ onto a track through woodland along The Holt. The track contours then descends to the rear of **Folkington** village. At a ✖ with the road through the village, keep ➜ and continue **SE** along the track. After 600m, the track bends **SW** and climbs for 1km, steeply at first, then more gradually to Teddard's Bottom before descending to a ✖. Turn ← and descend to the Jevington Road.

6 Turn ➜ onto the Jevington Road and continue for 750m through the village. Pass a dogleg ✖ after 650m and take the next ← onto the SDW. Begin the long, steady climb up the **W** spur of Bourne Hill, crossing the summit (201m) after 1.5km. Continue **SE** along the ridge on the SDW, looking down on Eastbourne to the **E**. Cross the A259 after 2.5km, then continue ⬆ before taking the ← fork (leaving the SDW) after 400m. Descend roughly **ESE** for 1km, initially on a grassy track, before arriving at the road by Paradise Plantation. Turn ➜ onto the road, bear ← after 300m and continue ⬆ over a ✖ before turning ← at a second ✖ after another 400m. Continue ⬆ for 1km to a roundabout, then turn ➜ for the train station and town centre.

Chalk bridleway track above Litlington

Climbing Bourne Hill from Jevington

Route 26

Eastbourne – Firle Beacon Circuit

26

START/FINISH	Eastbourne train station TV 610 991 or Warren Hill TV 588 979
DISTANCE	46km (28½ miles)
ON ROAD	8km (5 miles)
OFF ROAD	38km (23½ miles)
ASCENT	1195m (3920ft)
GRADE	◆
TIME	3hrs 30mins–4hrs
PUB	Various in Eastbourne and Alfriston
CAFÉ	The Hiker's Rest at East Dean; Charleston Farmhouse near Firle; The Beanstalk Teagarden, Old Coach Road by Firle

85% OFF ROAD

Overview

This is a tough and varied circular route, taking in Downland ridges, woodland tracks and picturesque villages, while enjoying expansive views across the Pevensey Levels, the Sussex Weald, the Cuckmere Valley and the English Channel. The route is mostly on bridleways and takes in sections of the South Downs Way (SDW) and the Weald Way (WW). There are seven major climbs: a 1km climb on a path and grassy slope from Paradise Plantation to Warren Hill at the start; a steady climb out of East Dean on the grassy slope of Hobb's Eares; a long steady climb over Snap Hill in Friston Forest, immediately followed by a 3.5km pull to the top of Windover Hill; a challenging climb up the steep northern escarpment of

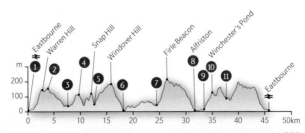

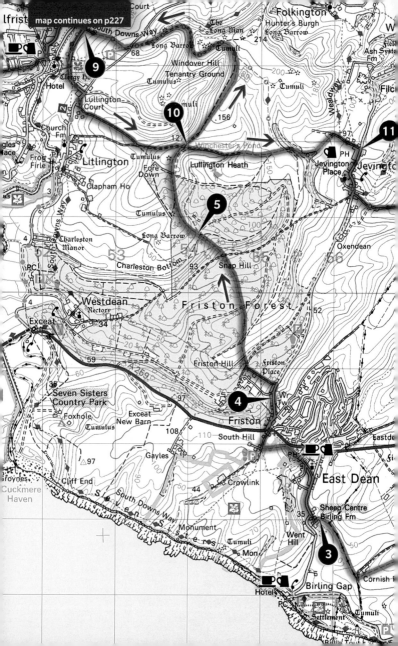

map continues on p227

Firle Beacon (the toughest on the route) and subsequent climbs to Winchester's Pond from Litlington and over Bourne Hill from Jevington, which will feel easy in comparison. Except the section through Friston Forest, which is prone to mud in winter, conditions are generally good. Watch out for walkers and horse riders – particularly along the SDW and WW sections.

Directions

1 From the station entrance, turn → and → again, arriving at a roundabout after 100m. Take the first ← (*Beachy Head*) and continue ↑ to pass the Law Courts and playing fields, keeping → then → again at a ✗ after 1km. Continue ↑ for 400m, going over a ✗ then taking the **RH** fork, arriving at Paradise Plantation after 300m. Turn ← onto a bridleway path. Climb roughly **WNW** for 700m, take the ← fork and continue climbing to a ✗. Swing ← (briefly joining the SDW) and continue to a ✗ with the `B2103`. Cross straight over the road to the **RH** fork and continue along Beachy Head Road for 500m, before turning → onto a bridleway (*Belle Tout Lighthouse 2 miles*).

Ⓐ There is a **car park** on the `B2103` just **N** of the top of Warren Hill that can be used as an alternative start point.

The gentle rolling landscape near East Dean

2 Descend, gently at first, then gather momentum along Long Down for 3km, before arriving to the rear of **Cornish Farm**. Go through two gates, cross a farm road to a confluence of signposts and gates, turn → through two gates and continue **NW** on a bridleway along a field edge. Pass through two gates along the way then descend to the rear of **Birling Farm**. Pass through a further two gates in quick succession and emerge onto the Birling Gap Road. Turn → to head **N** to East Dean.

3 After 600m, arrive at a fork and turn ← for **East Dean** village. Continue through the village, climbing along a narrow lane, then passing above the village green. Where the road bends, turn ← onto a concrete track, go through a gate and climb along bridleway on the steep grassy slope of Hobb's Eares. At the top of the slope, turn ← and make for the gate by the corner of a fenced paddock. Pass through, turn → and head for another gate 150m to the **W**. Go through and turn → onto a lane. Continue ↑ to emerge at the `A259` by Friston Church and pond.

4 Cross the `A259` and take the **LH** fork onto Jevington Road. Continue ↑ and take the ← fork after 200m. Continue ↑ and descend along the road for 400m, then take the second ← (private road, but signposted *public bridleway*) and descend the track road past **Friston Place**. At the next ✗ take the second → to climb through trees before crossing over the gallops on **Friston Hill** – be aware that **horses may be being exercised here** – and continue into Friston Forest on the far side. Continue along the bridleway, which is **prone to mud in winter**, descending to a ✗ after 500m. Continue ↑ and climb steadily up and over **Snap Hill**. The track levels out over Long Brow; continue ↑ over a ✗ before descending steeply to **Charleston Bottom** – keep → where the path forks halfway down.

5 This is a complicated ✗ – check the map! Take the **LH** option of two paths ↑ that climb **NW** and ascend steadily in a broad curve, arriving at a ✗ by **Winchester's Pond** after 1.4km. Dogleg ← then → and continue ↑ to climb initially **NE** before bending **NW** in a broad sweep, passing through three gates and reaching the top of **Windover Hill** (188m) after 2km. Continue ↑ then begin the fantastic curving descent on this excellent flint and chalk track at a sensible speed – **slow down** and give way to other users. Keep ← where the path forks halfway down. Pass through a gate and continue descending, then pass through another gate and cross ↑ over a road onto the SDW next to a car park. Descend for 700m on a steep, often slippery tree-lined track to emerge at a ✗. Continue ↑ along the road to cross the Cuckmere River on Long Bridge.

6 Turn → at the next ✗ to continue **N** on Alfriston Road for 100m before turning ← to climb gradually up the sunken road through **Winton**. This levels out and arrives at a ✗ after 600m. Turn → onto a farm track, then take the **LH** fork to continue along the Comp Lane track (Old Coach Road). Descend then climb a little past Comp Barn. Contour along with minor ups and downs beneath the northern escarpment of the Downs, keeping ↑ at all ✗s for nearly 5km, passing near Charleston Farmhouse before arriving at a ✘ in front of an old cottage with arched windows and Flemish bond brickwork. Take the second ← to stay on the Old Coach Road and continue to a ✘ at TQ 475 068.

House on the Old Coach Road

7 Turn ← and continue as the track leads to the **left** of woodland on an initially gentle gradient that soon begins to climb more steeply. Go through a gate after 500m and climb very steeply on a narrow, **often hoof-damaged** path. Pass through another gate as the path swings **ESE**, climbing along the escarpment. The path intersects with the SDW on top of the ridge. Continue ↑ through a gate and over the summit of **Firle Beacon** (217m) as the SDW bends **E** along the ridge. Drop down to pass Bopeep car park after 1km, passing through gates and climbing ↑ to pass over Bostal Hill. Continue ↑ for 1km past a ✘ and through a gate before beginning the 2.5km descent to **Alfriston**. Pass through two gates and continue ↑ over a ✘ after 1.2km; the path then becomes a broad chalk track (**can be very slippery in the wet**) that swings **S** and descends more steeply before joining a residential street as it enters Alfriston.

8 Follow the road to a ✘ and take the second → to arrive on Alfriston Road after 50m. Turn ← then continue ↑ before taking the **RH** fork past the old market cross to head **N** out of the village. After 500m turn → at a ✘ and continue across the Cuckmere River on Long Bridge.

To bail out from here, continue ↑ at the Cuckmere ✘ and cross the A27 to arrive at Berwick train station on the Eastbourne–Lewes line after 3.5km. This saves 10km.

Starting the descent to Jevington

9 At the next ✗ turn → and continue ↑ for 1km to another ✗. Turn → then, after 100m, turn ← onto a bridleway at TQ 525 026 and climb for 1km on a good track to a ✗. Turn → and continue to climb, arriving at a ✗ by **Winchester's Pond** after 600m.

10 Take the **LH** fork and continue ↑ to drop down then climb up across **Lullington Heath** and arrive at a ✗ after 1.5km. Go through the gate, continue ↑ over a ✗ and descend steeply through woodland – **watch out for walkers and horse riders**. Keep ← at a ✗ after 300m (the right-hand fork is the SDW, but this section is hemmed in by fences and often busy with walkers and horse riders). The path continues descending, bending **NE** then sharply **SE** before arriving at the ✗ with Jevington Road.

11 Turn → onto Jevington Road and continue for 750m through the village. Pass a dogleg ✗ after 650m and take the next ← onto the SDW. Begin the long steady climb up the **W** spur of Bourne Hill, crossing the summit (201m) after 1.5km. Continue **SE** along the ridge on the SDW, looking down on Eastbourne to the **E**. Cross the A259 after 2.5km and continue ↑ before taking the **LH** fork (leaving the SDW) after 400m. Descend roughly **ESE** for 1km, initially on grassy track, before arriving at the road by Paradise Plantation. Turn → onto the road, bear ← after 300m and continue ↑ over the next ✗ before turning ← at a second ✗ after another 400m. Continue ↑ for 1km to a roundabout and turn → for the train station and town centre.

Appendix A:
Camping and accommodation

The South Downs Way runs through cultivated land, unlike some other National Trails, so wild camping can be problematic. Legally you are not allowed to wild camp on any land without permission: however, if you are discreet, avoid crops, leave no litter and ask permission whenever possible most Sussex landowners will not object. Please do **not** light any fires.

There is a different landowner culture in Hampshire, perhaps because there are more commercial shooting estates, and you are unlikely to be able to wild camp here without being challenged.

Note that there is very little water in most suitable wild camping spots, so be prepared to collect and carry enough for your overnight needs en route (see Appendix B). Please do not try to wild camp on National Trust or Natural England land as you will be breaking the bylaws.

Campsites on the South Downs Way (W–E)
This list includes some campsites that are further away from the trail and so are more suitable for mountain bikers than for walkers. The distances given (in km) are the approximate distances from the SDW.

Morn Hill Caravan Site
Alresford Road
Chilcomb (2km) (Apr–Oct)
Tel: 01962 869877

Holden Farm
Cheriton, on trail (also barn)
Tel: 01962 771267

The Flowerpots Pub, Cheriton (3km)
camping at weekends only
Tel: 01962 771318

Oxenbourne Farm
East Meon (3km)
Tel: 01730 823239

The Sustainability Centre
Droxford Rd, East Meon, on trail
(open all year)
Tel: 01730 823549
hostel@sustainability-centre.org
www.sustainability-centre.org

New House Farm, East Dean (3km)
Tel: 01243 811685
Open from Easter throughout the summer weekends and at various other times through the season.

Graffham Camping/Caravanning Club Site
Great Bury, Graffham (3km) (Mar–Oct)
Tel: 01798 867476

Gumber Bothy Camping Barn
National Trust, Slindon Estate (1.5km)
(Mar–Oct) Tel: 01243 814484

Slindon Camping/Caravanning Club Site
Slindon Park (5km) (Mar–Oct)
Tel: 01243 814387

Houghton Farm, Houghton
Tel: 01798 831327 or 07710 630219

High Titten, High Titten Lane, Amberley
(on trail) (open all year)
informal camping area above Amberley at grid ref TQ 032 123. Free to use, covered shelter, but no water or toilets. This area does have a fire site you can use.

Washington Caravan and Camping Park
Washington (1km)
Tel: 01903 892869
washcamp@amserve.com

Buncton Manor Farm
Steyning Rd, Wiston (2km)
Tel: 01903 812736
bunctonmannor@tiscali.co.uk

White House Caravan Site, Newham Lane
Steyning (1km) (Mar–Nov)
Tel: 01903 813737

Farmhouse Caravan and Camp Site
Tottington Drive, Small Dole (2km)
Tel: 01273 493157

Downsview Caravan Park
Woodmancote (4km) (Apr–Oct)
Tel: 01273 492801

Wanbarrow Farm, Bullfinch Lane
Hurstpierpoint (4km) (also barn)
Tel: 01273 834110
ninajarman@hotmail.com

Southdown Way Caravan and Camping
Park, Southdown Farm, Lodge Lane
Keymer (2km) (Easter–October)
Tel: 01273 841877
site@southdown-caravancamping.org.uk

Sandown Caravan Park, Streat (2km)
(Apr–Sept) Tel: 01273 890035

Blackberry Woods Streat Lane
Streat (2km) Tel: 01273 890035
www.blackberrywood.com

The Plough Inn, Plumpton Green
(4km) Tel: 01273 890311
scooby976@supanet.com

The Half Moon Pub, Lewes Rd
Plumpton (1.5km)
Tel: 01273 890253

Hackmans Farm, Lewes Road
Plumpton (1.5km) (Mar–Oct)
Tel: 01273 890348

Spring Barn Farm, Kingston Rd
Kingston (2.5km)

Itford Farm, Beddingham, near Lewes
(on trail) Tel: 01273 85843
murraybricknell@supanet.com

Pleasant Rise Farm, Cuckmere Road
Alfriston (on trail) Tel: 01323 734265
info@alfristoncamping.co.uk
www.alfristoncamping.co.uk

Ash Farm, Filching, Jevington (1km)
Tel: 01323 487335
geof@onetel.net

Foxhole campsite and camping barn
Seven Sisters Country Park, Exceat
(On non-bridleway section of SDW)
(open 1 April–31 October)
Tel: 01323 870280
sevensisters@southdowns-aonb.gov.uk
www.sevensisters.org.uk
For pre-arranged educational groups and
events only

Buckle Caravan Park, Marine Parade
Seaford (8km to footpath route)
Tel: 01323 897801

Fairfields Farm Caravan and Camping Park
Westham, near Pevensey (8km)
Tel: 01323 763165
enquiries@fairfieldsfarm.com
www.fairfieldsfarm.com

Youth Hostels

You cannot camp at most of these hostels
but they do offer an economical alternative
where camping is not an option. Breakfast
and evening meals are usually available.

For more information on any of the YHA
hostels, for availability and bookings visit
www.yha.org.uk.

Weatherdown Hostel, The Sustainability
Centre, Droxford Road, East Meon (on
trail) (open all year) £23–£30 with breakfast (camping also available)

Tel: 01730 823549
hostel@sustainability-centre.org

Truleigh Hill YHA, Truleigh Hill
near Shoreham-by-Sea (on trail)
(open all year) £16 Tel: 0870 7706078
truleigh@yha.org.uk

Telscombe YHA, Telscombe Village (3km)
£18 Tel: 0870 7706062

South Downs YHA, Itford Farm
Beddingham, near Lewes (on trail)
(open all year) £16 Tel: 0845 371 9574
southdowns@yha.org.uk

Alfriston YHA, Frog Firle, near Alfriston
(0.5km to SDW footpath, 1.2km to SDW
bridleway) (open all year) £17
Tel: 0870 7705666
alfriston@yha.org.uk

Note that the old Winchester YHA is now
closed.

Eastbourne YHA, East Dean Road
Eastbourne (0.5km from SDW)
(26 March–14 Oct) £18.50
Tel: 0845 3719316
eastbourne@yha.org.uk

Other 'MTB-friendly' accommodation

Below is a brief list of 'MTB-friendly' bed
and breakfast accommodation on or near
the SDW.

There are many more 'MTB-friendly' bed
and breakfasts and hotels within striking
distance of the SDW. Visit www.nationaltrail.
co.uk/south-downs-way/accommodation
for a comprehensive list.

12 Christchurch Road
Winchester, Hampshire SO23 9SR (1km)
Tel: 01962 854272

5 Compton Road,
Winchester, Hampshire SO23 9SL (1km)
Tel: 01962 869199
www.winchesterbedandbreakfast.net

80 Rushes Road
Petersfield, Hampshire, GU32 3BP (5km)
Tel: 01730 261638
www.rushes-road.co.uk

Border Cottage, 4 Heath Road
Petersfield, Hampshire GU31 4DU (5km)
Tel: 01730 263179
www.bordercottage.co.uk

Copper Beeches
Torberry Farm, Hurst, Nr Petersfield,
Hampshire GU31 5RG
Tel: 01730 826662
www.copperbeeches.net

Moonlight Cottage
Cocking, West Sussex GU29 0HN (1km)
Tel: 01730 810102
www.moonlightcottage.co.uk

Selden Farm, Selden Lane
Patching, West Sussex BN13 3UL
Tel: 01903 871672
www.seldenfarm.co.uk

Riverside House, Houghton Bridge
Amberley, West Sussex BN18 9LP
Tel: 01798 831066

Long Island, School Lane
Washington, West Sussex RH20 4AP (1km)
Tel: 01903 892237

Hobbs Cottage, South Downs Way
Pyecombe, West Sussex BN45 7EG
(on trail) Tel: 01273 846150

Tovey Lodge, Underhill Lane
Ditchling, East Sussex BN6 8XE (1km)
Tel: 01273 256156
www.sussexcountryholidays.co.uk

The Dairy, Spring Barn Farm
Kingston Road, Kingston, Nr Lewes,
Sussex BN7 3ND
Tel: 07867 790972
www.thedairyspringbarn.com

The Silverdale, 21 Sutton Park Road
Seaford, East Sussex BN25 1RH (3km)
Tel: 01323 491849

The Guesthouse East, 13 Hartington Place
Eastbourne, East Sussex BN21 3BS (2km)
Tel: 01323 722774
www.theguesthouseeast.co.uk

Beachy Rise Guest House
5 Beachy Head Road, Eastbourne
East Sussex BN20 7QN (0.5km)
Tel: 01323 639171

Appendix B:

Water points along the South Downs Way

Some taps may be drained and turned off between November and March to prevent pipes freezing and bursting. Some of the water points listed below are at pubs, hence water is only available during opening hours. Listed from West to East, water points (with map references) are available at:

The Milburys (pub) SU 570 246

Lomer Farm (tap) SU 590 237

The Shoe Inn, Exton (pub) SU 614 209

Meon Springs, Whitewool Farm
SU 655 215. Water available from the fishing lodge when open.

Queen Elizabeth Country Park (tap and café) SU 718 185 (café open 9–5 most of the year, check opening times in winter Tel: 023 92591362)

Hill Barn, A286 crossing
(tap and trough) SU 879 166

Amberley, near river Arun crossing
(tap and trough) TQ 025 124

Franklin Arms, Washington (pub)
TQ 123 129

Parkfield Farm, Washington, A24 crossing
(tap) TQ 118 119

Botolphs, River Adur crossing
(tap and trough) TQ 198 094

Truleigh Hill (Tottington Barn) YHA
(outside tap) TQ 220 106

Devil's Dyke (pub) TQ 258 110

Saddlescombe Farm (tap) TQ 271 114

The Downland Church of the Transfiguration, Pyecombe (kitchen with tap and tea/coffee facilities; also WC)
TQ 292 126

Housedean Farm, A27 crossing
(tap) TQ 368 092

Southease Church (tap) TQ 423 052

Itford Farm YHA (tap & café,
from Spring 2011) TQ 433 056

Alfriston village (several pubs and public toilets but no trough) TQ 520 030

The Eight Bells, Jevington (pub)
TQ 562 017

Appendix C:
Bike shops/mechanics

Peter Hansford
91 Olivers Battery Rd South
Winchester, Hampshire SO22 4JQ
Tel: 01962 877555
www.peterhansford.co.uk

Hargroves Cycles Ltd
Unit 1, Winchester Trade Park,
Easton Lane, Winchester, Hampshire
SO23 7FA
Tel: 01962 840707
www.hargrovescycles.co.uk

Owens Cycles
22 Lavant Street, Petersfield
Hampshire GU32 3EN
Tel: 01730 260446
www.owenscycles.co.uk

Cycleworks
21 Chapel Street, Petersfield
Hampshire GU32 3DT
Tel: 01730 263370
www.cycleworks.co.uk

Cyclelife Petersfield
Rear 40 Dragon Street, Petersfield
Hampshire GU31 4JJ
Tel: 01730 266644
www.cyclelife.com

South Downs Bikes
38 West Street, Storrington
West Sussex RH20 4EE
Tel: 01903 745534
www.southdownsbikes.com

MSG Bikes
20 Crabtree Lane, Lancing
West Sussex BN15 9PQ
Tel: 01903 752308
www.msgbikes.com

Raleigh Cyclelife Centre
38–42 Kingston Broadway
Shoreham-by-Sea
West Sussex BN43 6TE
Tel: 01273 596368
www.cyclelife.com

M's Cycles
60 High Street, Shoreham-by-Sea
BN43 5DB
Tel: 01273 567591
www.mscycles.co.uk

Baker Street Bikes
7–8 York Place, Brighton
East Sussex BN1 4GU
Tel: 01273 675754
www.bakerstbikes.co.uk

Sydney Street Bikes
24 Sydney St, North Lanes
Brighton, East Sussex BN1 4EN
Tel: 01273 624700

Rayment Cycles
13/14 Circus Parade
New England Road
Brighton, East Sussex BN1 4GW
Tel: 01273 697617
www.rayment-cycles.co.uk

Lewes Cycle Shack
53 Cliffe High Street
Lewes, East Sussex BN7 2AN
Tel: 01273 479688
www.lewescycleshack.co.uk

Lewes Cycle Shack (was FutureCycles)
39a Friars Walk
Lewes, East Sussex BN7 2LG
Tel: 01273 483108

Mr Cycles Ltd
26 Clinton Place
Seaford, East Sussex BN25 1NP
Tel: 01323 893130
www.mrcycles.co.uk

Cuckmere Cycle Co. Ltd
The Granary Barn
Seven Sisters Country Park
Exceat, East Sussex BN25 4AD
Tel: 01323 870310
www.cuckmere-cycle.co.uk

The Tri Store
49 Grove Road, Eastbourne
East Sussex, BN21 4TX
www.thetristore.com

Heath Cycles
106 Cavendish Place
Eastbourne
East Sussex BN21 3TZ
Tel: 01323 733404

Cycleman
46 Rosebery Avenue
Hampden Park
Eastbourne, East Sussex BN22 9QB
Tel: 01323 501157

Phoenix Cycles
217–219 Seaside
Eastbourne, East Sussex BN22 7NR
Tel: 01323 729060
www.phoenixcycles.co.uk

Appendix D:

Useful contacts

South Downs National Park Authority
South Downs Centre,
North Street, Midhurst,
West Sussex GU29 9DH
Tel: 01730 814810
www.southdowns.gov.uk

Public transport and accommodation

For train timetable information and to book tickets online:
www.nationalrail.co.uk.
For National Rail Enquiries:
Tel: 08457 484950.

For comprehensive information on transport, accommodation and plenty of other useful content for visitors to the South Downs, visit www.nationaltrail.co.uk/southdowns.

South Downs area mountain biking clubs, associations and websites

Hampshire
www.southdownsmtb.co.uk
www.newforce.org.uk
mad-dogs-winchester.webs.com
www.fareham-wheelers.org.uk

West Sussex
www.vttexplorers.co.uk
www.dirt-devils.fsnet.co.uk
rubberhatmtb.com

East Sussex
www.southdownsmountainbiking.co.uk
brightonmtb.org
www.mtbbrighton.com
www.eastbournerovers.com
mtb-nomads.blogspot.com

Other South Downs mountain biking websites
www.bikedowns.co.uk
www.mtbdiary.co.uk
www.southdownsdouble.net

Listing of Cicerone Guides

For full information on all our guides,
books and eBooks, visit our website:
www.cicerone.co.uk

Walking – Trekking – Mountaineering – Climbing – Cycling

Over 40 years, Cicerone have built up an outstanding collection of over 300 guides, inspiring all sorts of amazing adventures.

 Every guide comes from extensive exploration and research by our expert authors, all with a passion for their subjects. They are frequently praised, endorsed and used by clubs, instructors and outdoor organisations.

All our titles can now be bought as **e-books**, **ePubs** and **Kindle** files and we also have an online magazine – **Cicerone Extra** – with features to help cyclists, climbers, walkers and trekkers choose their next adventure, at home or abroad.

Our website shows any **new information** we've had in since a book was published. Please do let us know if you find anything has changed, so that we can publish the latest details. On our **website** you'll also find great ideas and lots of detailed information about what's inside every guide and you can buy **individual routes** from many of them online.

It's easy to keep in touch with what's going on at Cicerone by getting our monthly **free e-newsletter**, which is full of offers, competitions, up-to-date information and topical articles. You can subscribe on our home page and also follow us on **Facebook** and **Twitter** or dip into our **blog**.

Cicerone – the very best guides for exploring the world.

CICERONE

Juniper House, Murley Moss, Oxenholme Road, Kendal, Cumbria LA9 7RL
Tel: 015395 62069 info@cicerone.co.uk
www.cicerone.co.uk and **www.cicerone-extra.com**